A CANDLE
IN THE GRUB BOX

The story of Frank Jackson as told to Sheila Douglass.

i

To the memory of Louise Barr Jackson.

Standard Book No. 0-919213-68-5

Published by
Shires Books
246 Seafield Rd.
Victoria, B.C. V9S 1S6

Printing and Typesetting by
Friesen Printers
209-5752 176th St.
Vancouver, B.C.
Head Office: Altona, Man.

Introduction

After listening to Frank Jackson's after-dinner stories, we all used to say, he should write a book. But Frank, although eighty was too busy living in the present to write a book about what was past. So I sneakily taped about eight hours of his stories, spent the winter transcribing them into chapters and took them back to him on my next visit. His only comment after reading them was, "That's all wrong!"

As it happened asthma clipped his wings somewhat, so he started to write a blow by blow account of his life during the last fifty years. When he went to read it over he couldn't read his writing, so he left me to decipher and transcribe. I have deciphered, transcribed, chopped up and rearranged, but I have tried to leave this account the way Frank wrote it — an understatement. You will have to use your imagination to realize the predicament he was in when injured in the bush miles from home and in forty below weather. In the words of his wife, Dr. Mary Percy Jackson,

"His safe arrival at Isidore's camp was a near miracle, and a remarkable feat of endurance, and his dogs were really something out of the ordinary, that they would stand at the top of the river bank and wait for him to struggle up the hill!" You will have to imagine the horror of those flies, and the emotion he felt when tragedy hit; and you will have to go and stand on the top of Naylor Hills to realize the vastness of this north country, which Frank so nonchalantly travelled over.

A romanticized account of his life would never have got past Frank, for such books, he thinks are nonsense, and he cannot understand how anyone can write them. When I read this account to Frank, his comment was,

"Yes, that's how it was." However, he insists that if there are any mistakes, they are mine and not his!

A special appeal: — If you have old letters and photographs which illustrate our past, please, please, please, do not throw them out but donate them to your local museum or archives. Letters which Frank wrote over fifty years were destroyed even while we were putting together this book. Photographs which the Jacksons had kindly lent to various authors over the years were never returned, so we have done the best we could with what was left, plus the help of the Peace River Centennial Museum, the Archives of British Columbia and the Glenbow-Alberta Institute, for which we say thankyou.

Sheila M. Douglass,
Nanaimo, B.C., September/77

Rainbow Lake

High Level

Ft. Vermilion

Ft. Chipewayan

Peace River

Keg River

Carcajou

Athabasca River

Notikewin

Fairview

Peace River

Grimshaw

Lesser Slave Lake

Slave Lake

Smoky River

Athabasca

Jarvie

WesHock

North Saskatchewan River

R O C K I E S

Edmonton

Red Deer
Lake

Ferintosh

Doren Lee

Bashaw

Red Deer River

Drumheller

Bow River

Badlands

Calgary

The area covered by this <u>rough</u>
sketch map is <u>approx</u> 900 miles north to south,
by 500 miles east to west. For those who think
that Edmonton is in northern Alberta,
Athabasca is <u>approx</u>. halfway between
the north and south borders!

South Saskatchewan River

Medicine Hat

Table of Contents

CHAPTER ONE

Medicine Hat

I was born in Southend, England, where my father owned and managed a big plumbing, heating, and decorating business left to him by his father. When he sold that we lived in a big country house on the Isle of Thanet in Kent, where my mother had plenty of servants to do the work, and my father found plenty of time to play cricket. My sisters and I were taught by a Miss Cross and I sang in the church choir.

I remember going to Ramsgate to see Buffalo Bill's Wild West Show, it poured with rain, and driving home in an open rig we got really wet. Sometimes we went up to London to visit the Hippodrome or the Coliseum. The circus ring at the Hippodrome could be lowered and filled with water, and I remember seeing a show there with eighty polar bears swimming around and sliding down a slide. As well as Dad's income Mother owned property, but they lost everything, and so decided to come to Canada.

I left England with my dad on March 10, 1904. On the boat we ran into terrific storms and I was really sick. I went up on deck, snugged up a little hole for myself, and crawled in. The sailors were battening everything down, and chasing people below. One of them caught sight of me, and hauled me out by the scruff of the neck.

"What the devil do you think you're doing?,' he yelled. I tried to tell him that I was resting, but he didn't listen as he hustled me below. That's all I recollect about the boat trip, but I do remember having to stop off in Winnipeg, and having a hard time to walk up the street, the mud was pretty near up to my waist!

On May 24, 1904, my mother and three sisters, Grace, 'Bert', and Dot, left England for Canada. They carried a caged canary with them, and it sang all the way across Canada on the train. We were all bound for Medicine Hat in Alberta, because Dad knew some folks there.

In Medicine Hat Dad went to work as a Sanitary Inspector for the Canadian Pacific Railway. The first year, the girls all went to school. I should have gone to school but I thought I would be better off earning some money, so I got a job in Mitchell Marshall's hardware store. Working in the store taught me a lot; I was tinsmith, storeclerk, delivery boy, I did anything and everything there was to do.

After about two years someone realized that I ought to be in school, and the Inspector came round, he said I had to go to school and learn something. I told him I was learning every day in the store and getting paid for it. He said, maybe so, but the law said, I had to go to school. It was examination time, so I told him that I would go and write the Grade Nine exams, and if I didn't pass I would go to school!

The High School was a new brick building at the top of a hill, about three miles from home. I went to school for two weeks, riding there on Grace's bicycle. I had to walk up the hills as they were too steep to ride. All the other kids were older and bigger than I was except Paddy Russell, her dad was a conductor on the railroad, she was fourteen too, we both passed the exams, and that was the end of my school career!

Grace got married, Bert went to Normal School in Calgary, and eventually Dot left school. I was having trouble with my chest, Dr. Woodland, our doctor, thought this was caused by the fumes from the acids used in the tinsmith's shop, so he advised me to leave the store. They did everything to persuade me to stay, but I couldn't stand working inside any longer, so I left.

I went to work for Jim Mitchell of the Z-T ranch. I was about fourteen and I couldn't ride a horse, but I used to tally and they gave us gentle horses to begin with. No-one taught me to ride, I just hung on, and learned by experience. I lived at the ranch, where we had breakfast about five o'clock, were at work by six, and didn't quit working until sunset. The pay was $30 a month with no days off. There was always plenty to do.

We started with the spring roundup. The ranchers worked together, sending a representative or rep for each ranch, or one man could rep two small ranches. One man, generally a rancher, acted as captain or boss. We took a chuckwagon driven by the cook, and a bedwagon carrying the tents and bedrolls, driven by the nightherder. We also hauled firewood, as there was very little wood on the prairies. The low hills were covered with sagebrush, a few cottonwood trees grew along the river's edge, and willows, chokecherries, and pincherries grew in the steep-sided valleys we call coulees.

It was usual to move every day to a different watering place, I was dayherder for about a hundred head of saddlehorses, I would take over at daylight and look after them until dark. The rider would tell me which horse to ride, a different one every day. We were camped at Many Island Lake, when the rider gave me a horse that had a nasty habit of rearing over backwards when I tried to turn him or pull him up. Harry Bray said to the rider,

"You shouldn't have given that horse to the kid, I'm going to teach him a lesson." Harry rode the horse on the beach, where he had found an old whisky bottle which was full of sand.

"Every time he rears over backwards, I'm going to give him a swipe with the bottle," said Harry. He did and the horse dropped dead! In those days there were lots of horses, you could buy a horse for ten dollars and we had about six hundred of them on the ranch.

On one roundup Harry Bray was thrown from his horse and injured, the captain told me to go down to the camp and look at him. The cook had put mustard poultices on him which gave him huge blisters. I had a look, I could feel that he had broken a collar bone, I told the captain, who told me to take him to town which was 35-40 miles away, but Harry said he could manage alone and he did. Harry's father was Sergeant Major J. H. G. Bray the second man to enlist in the Northwest Mounted Police at Toronto in 1873.

2

If mange became prevalent in the summer then every animal in the country had to be dipped. Mange is a parasite, and it spreads rapidly. The dipping vat was at Mitchells, so the cattle were rounded up there. It took us three or four weeks to round up nineteen thousand cattle, and three or four days to put them through the vat.

It needed about twenty riders to hold them down on the flat, there were a series of corrals, a big one holding about fifty head, then a smaller one holding fifteen or twenty head at the head of the chute. The floor of the chute where they entered the dipping vat, was of sheet iron the width of a cow, and once they stepped onto it they shot into the vat because they had no footing. They had to swim through the vat and be dipped right underneath the water, we daren't miss a single spot. When an animal has mange, its hide itches and if they can find a place to rub against, they'll rub themselves raw, it's terrible.

The Dominion Government Vet, Dr. Jack Hargrave, who was also Jim Mitchell's brother-in-law, was there to supervise the dipping vat, making sure that the waterlevel was kept up, and the temperature to about 90 degrees F. The dip contained sulphur, so you can imagine what it was like with hot, smelly steam rising from the vat all the time, you could smell it for miles. The water was heated in an old upright boiler fired by coal, with pipes running from the boiler into the dipping vat. If the water got too hot we had to haul half a dozen barrels of water from the river to cool it down.

The cattle climbed out of the vat into a dripping pen that held about ten head; the water dripped off them and ran back into the vat. Then they were turned into another corral and eventually the brandreader turned them loose.

Mennonites had moved into the district and were living on the benches of the South Saskatchewan River in a place called Happy Land. They had no money to buy lumber, and there were no trees, so they lived in sod houses, some of them were just holes in the ground roofed over with sods. They all had two or three milk cows, and when the men were out on the circle rounding up the cattle, they had to roundup these cows too.

To control mange every single head of cattle in the country had to be dipped. After being dipped, the Mennonite's cattle were turned loose with the others, and being forty or so miles from home had no idea how to get back. The homesteaders hadn't the know-how to find their way around; the range cattle always go back to their range, but milk cows will park wherever they can find feed. It was tough on those fellows, some of their cattle weren't found until a year later when they were dry and no good for milk cows. It was the job of the range-rider to go round and discover any calves or cattle that were tied up, and report them to Hargrave who would send someone round to hand-dip them.

It was while we were dipping that I injured my knee for the first time. I was tallying on one side and Jack Hargrave was tallying on the other side; the cattle came up a chute out of the dip, and as they came up, whichever side the brand was on, the person at that side read it and marked it down, then we had a record of whose cattle we were dipping.

There were no flies but it was terribly hot; we ran out of cattle, they were all milling around down on the river flat, and the men were having a hard time. Working in the corrals, on foot in the dust, herding cattle into different

3

pens, was a terrible job; tallying was better for we were above the cattle. We waited for quite a while, then Hargrave said,

"They seem to be having lots of trouble down there, maybe we should go and help." A team was standing by that were used to haul water from the river for the dipping vat, one was a bay, and the other was a sorrel, there were also two saddles lying around, so I said, "Let's go!" Jack saddled up the bay horse and took off for the river.

I saddled up the sorrel and he just stood there quietly. I was a passable rider by this time, and I thought they were broken saddle horses, but they weren't, at least mine wasn't. I got on, and he took off like a bullet. He ran round and round the corral crowding me against the rails, catching my knee on the little posts that stuck out of the rails, and smashing up my kneecap.

On the way to the river Hargrave met the boys coming up with a bunch of cattle. When they got back, I was still lying on the ground where I had fallen. The boss, Mitchell came up and looked at me.

"What are you trying to do? Make a damn fool of yourself? I hired plenty of them already!" That's all the sympathy I got!

"You needn't worry," I said, and got up on my feet. I stood up there on one leg and tallied all day. I've had my knee operated on three times, but it's always been a darn nuisance.

There was big territory to cover on a roundup in the days before there were fences, when a man or a company could hold leases of up to 100,000 acres of Crown lands from the Dominion Government, for which they paid one cent per acre per year in rent. The captain knew where the cattle were, each herd had its own stamping ground, usually a ten mile radius round a slough hole. A slough hole is a depression in the ground where melted snow collects in the spring. When the men went out in the morning, the captain would tell them which circle to take, they went in two's, and it could be a long circle or a short circle.

In the fall roundup we branded calves and took out the beef. Beef roundups usually ended at Many Island Lake ready to ship them at Ft. Walsh. We had a fire in the open for branding, there'd be two men catching calves, roping them by the hind feet. They would bring them in just as fast as we could brand them, they were top-notch ropers. I was no good at roping feet, but I could catch anything by the neck. If a man wanted a saddle horse out of a bunch, even if they were milling around, I could always catch him. But those fellows were catching calves by the hind feet with hundreds of head milling around in there, and they rarely missed, they were sure good.

Previously there had been no farmers in the west, and those that did come in took up land close to the railroad, but by 1908 and 1909, farmers started taking up land encroaching on the open range. This interfered with the ranchers, who then had to depend on leases, which had to be fenced, to hold the stock.

A native called Lawrence worked for us; he used to break horses to drive, and when he wasn't doing that he used to fix fences. Our fence wasn't on survey, it ran up and down through the sandhills in as straight a line as possible, but if a man took up a homestead straddling our fence then we had to move the fence back. Lawrence would put the fence posts up, and I would

4

unroll the wire by hand; this was too slow and too much work, so I had to find an easier way of unrolling the wire.

With an eight foot spool and a hay rake, I invented a contraption that could be pulled by a team. The spool acted as a wheel and we could put six or seven hundred pounds of wire on it. When it was too far to roll the spool, we used a stoneboat to drag it to where we wanted it, and it worked fine.

We had a blacksmith's shop on the ranch, and I got a man named Joe Bush, who was a Cossack, to help me bend the angle iron as I wasn't strong enough. We had to have a fire outside as we couldn't handle it in the forge.

We didn't have a regular blacksmith on the ranch but Joe knew how to shoe horses, I watched him and then practised myself. I found there was nothing to it, once I'd watched it being done. Joe was quite handy, and he was darn good at halter-breaking horses. I was no good at that, I tried and tried and tried to halter-break horses, but Joe would have them following him all over, before mine would even slack up on the rope. It's a real knack to top off those broncs.

The ranchers struggled along with their fenced leases, but they had troubles. For instance, they might fence a whole township for a winter pasture and keep the stock off it in the summer, but according to the law, if hay wasn't cut by the first of October, the hay permit was automatically cancelled, and anybody could go and cut it. So homesteaders would go and cut a fellow's winter pasture for hay. There was hell-a-popping for a year or two, but the ranchers couldn't do anything about it.

The homesteaders took up more and more land, and the fenced leases were not large enough to run the herds the ranchers had been used to keeping, so they had to cut down. As there was now no open range to speak of, there was no longer any need for the big roundups.

The ranchers couldn't expect to hold the country forever. The land was all over-grazed, and when winter came and there wasn't enough feed, cattle died. Under the present system we've got twice as many cattle in Alberta.

Dad decided to get a homestead, and his friend, L. B. Cochrane told him he knew of one. I went with Dad one Sunday to see it, it was winter-time and we crossed the river on the ice. The homestead was on the river flat, alongside Hargrave's place, and there was nothing on it but cactus and sagebrush between the rocks. Next time they met, Cochrane asked Dad if he'd been to see the homestead. Dad told him he wasn't interested in the place for nothing would grow there.

"You should take it up," said Cochrane. "One day they'll do away with that ferry and put a bridge in there." But Dad wouldn't listen to him. Dr. Woodland filed on it and proved it up. Cochrane was right, before we left the 'Hat', the bridge was built across onto that property, and it was sold for $160,000. Dad had refused to give ten dollars for it!

Instead, Dad took up a homestead not far from Mitchell's lease fence about seven miles from Medicine Hat. He built a house on this and Mother lived there with Dot. Dad came home periodically when he could get away from his work. I had bought a few cows from time to time, and, as riding for Mitchell became less on account of confining cattle within fences, I stayed at my Dad's place to look after my cows.

Vincent Minnizisky ran the Maple Leaf Dairy, he was a Cossack, used as an interpreter by the Northwest Mounted Police, he also hunted wolves for bounty. The dairy was about two miles north of us, and they passed our place on their way to Medicine Hat to deliver their milk. I made a deal with Minnizisky to buy my milk for 5¢ a quart, which was cheap, and this arrangement went on for two years. Then he came and told me he was getting too old to carry on and was going to quit. He suggested I take it over, which I did. What a headache!

First I had to build a barn which had to have concrete floors to comply with regulations for dairy barns. Dot and I used to get up at 4 a.m. to milk twenty cows. While I washed, shaved, dressed, and ate breakfast, Dot would harness the team, and Mother would bottle the milk. I would then deliver the milk around the town and Dot would finish up in the barn and put the cows out.

Sometimes Dot would get another team ready for when I came back, and I'd go out and plow some ground until it got dark. In the summertime I might take out another milk round at night. When I brought back the empty bottles, they all had to be washed. It was hard work; you scarcely had time to go to bed! We ran that dairy for several years. I sold out, but the buyers went broke, and I never got paid. So we ran it again for another year, and sold out again, the same thing happened, so finally we quit.

Farmers really started to move in, but there was no rain and no snow, and as the land was plowed, it started to blow away. A man from Idaho brought in two big steam outfits and bought land all over. His crops failed, and he borrowed money to put in more crops, he put in six or seven crops in succession and they all failed. All that machinery was no good without rain.

We did have a crop one year and we couldn't get anyone to thresh it. We had to put a sheaf in a sack, rub it off, then lay it out on the table and pick out the grain. The last year we were there, the crop failed to grow at all, and one year we planted potatoes and took up the same potatoes in the fall!

The wind was terrible. It could blow all day and all night for six or seven days at a stretch. We anchored the wagon when we left it, with an iron pin driven into the ground, otherwise we might not have found it when we came back.

We planted trees to break the wind, different kinds of poplar and ash, they grew quite big, but after we left, the sand blew in and buried their roots four or five feet deep, and they all died.

We had saved all our calves and were getting quite a herd, it was impossible to keep them on the pasture we had and buy feed for the winter, so it was decided that I would go off, and look for a suitable place where we could have pasture and put up hay for the winter.

I finally found a place I thought was suitable. I bought a section of C.P.R. land on Red Deer Lake, about thirty miles east of Wetaskiwin. My Dad wanted to retire because of ill health, so I bought a half-section of homestead land for my folks from a Norwegian bachelor who wanted to return to Norway. This land was in poplar country, and sure looked good after the bald-headed prairie.

Frank, at home writing his memoirs.

We lived in a big country house on the Isle of Thanet in Kent.

Frank and his family, as a boy in England.

Frank sang in the church choir.

CHAPTER TWO

Trail Through The Badlands

I returned to Medicine Hat and informed my folks of what I had done. We decided that I should leave with all the young stock and horses, and go overland to the new location. I faced a drive of about two hundred miles over sparsely populated country. Quite a prospect!

It was early summer when I set off, accompanied by a young lad called Percy Wills who drove the team. He was from the Welsh mountains, I was always given to understand that the Welsh could speak English but this boy was harder to understand than a Scotsman!

After crossing the South Saskatchewan River, we headed northwest towards the Red Deer River. We had a difficult time after we left Redcliffe, irrigation ditches were being dug, and there were no bridges, so we had to wander north to get around them. At last we left the ditches behind, but the next problem was to find water for the stock, and one time we went for two days without finding any.

I was riding a white mare who put her foot in a badger hole and broke her leg. The skin was not broken, fortunately, so as there was no chance of forming, 'proud flesh', I splinted it with chokecherry and bandaged it. It healed up; although she was always lame after this — she produced two or three good colts.

The horse attended to, I was now on foot, and somehow had to catch another saddle horse. I couldn't rope one from one of the workhorses for they weren't fast enough, so I rode a workhorse down a trail for twelve miles driving the horses in front of me, until we came to a ranch where I coralled them and roped one.

Finally we made the Red Deer River, expecting to water our thirsty stock, but we were in the badlands and between us and the water were steep, weathered cliffs, with no apparent way down. We made another dry camp on the top bench that night. After supper I decided to explore a coulee, hoping to find water, I didn't find water, but as darkness fell, I found the coulee to be full of fireflies, a beautiful sight!

At daylight we found we were on foot, our picket horse had gone with all the rest. There was a wagon trail going west from where we were camped, and finding horse tracks on it, I followed them. I tracked them for four or five miles until I came to a big valley. On the far side I saw a ranch house with a bunch of horses close by: I recognized some of these horses as mine, as I had three white horses in the bunch.

When I arrived at the ranch, the rancher was just coming out of the house with a pail of hot water. After I'd explained about our horses, he told me to come to the barn and he would show me how lucky I was. In the barn were two mares that had been attacked by wolves, they were sure torn up with holes in their hind legs. We agreed that the wolves must have scared my horses, chased them down the trail to his place, where they had run through his mares and caught two of them.

The rancher told me how difficult these wolves were to hunt in the Badlands, the Cattleman's Association paid a hundred dollar bounty on them, and Indians from the Gleichen Reserve hunted them, but with little success. He invited me to bring my stock to his place to water, and also told me where the trail to the river lay, but suggested that I leave it until the next day to follow, as it was a long, bad trail. I caught a horse and rode back to camp.

We arrived at the ranch and watered the cattle. Close to the buildings there was a drinking trough supplied with water from an artesian well. The water flowed in a steady stream down the long trough where the cattle drank, and into the valley. I was told that it flowed like that winter and summer alike. I decided to night herd the animals and we got through the night with no more visits from wolves. At daylight we pulled out.

The trail down to the river was sure some trail, it must have been from ten to twelve miles long, dropping from one bench to another and heading in all directions. About two miles before we hit the river we found a small deserted ranch in a coulee, a beautiful place, with balm of gileads, chokecherry trees, saskatoons, and different kinds of fruit growing there. Way up in the hillside there was a spring, and the rancher had built a trough to harness it, the water was about an inch deep and just racing down the trough. He had put in pipes to the house for his water supply, and a small waterwheel about a foot wide was fastened to a shaft connected to an old car generator. There were wires going to the house for power, and the light near the generator still worked. It was obvious that no-one had lived there for a 'coon's age, but it was a beautiful place, so unexpected in this dry country.

It was sundown before we finally reached the river's bank and found a place to camp. The rancher told me that upstream from where the trail hit the river, there was a place where we could ford the river with a wagon. At daylight the next morning we found out how wrong he was. As it hadn't been raining we were surprised to find the river was so full. We drove our wagon into the water, and almost immediately the lead horse was almost swimming, and the wagon was so tilted, I thought we were going to lose horses and wagon in the river.

I swung the lead team back, and Wills got into the water and managed to unhook the double trees and get the horses out. We put them on behind to pull the wagon out of the river and up the hill again, it was impossible for them to back it up, as the bank was too steep. The river was full enough to carry a steamboat, and impossible to ford, so I rode further up the river to see what else I could find.

Two or three miles upstream I found better pasture, so we moved and made camp. Further still upstream, I found a ferry cable across the river, there was no ferry to be seen, but it looked as if it had been in use recently. I could also see some buildings across the river, in a coulee just below the hills, but no sign of life, so I went back to camp for lunch.

12

After lunch I decided to ride up the valley with Wills to see what we could find. I forget how far we rode, but eventually we found a little store, here we met Drumheller. He told us that they had had very heavy rains west of Red Deer which accounted for the river being in flood. I asked him about the ferry cable, and he told me that there was usually a ferry there, and he thought they would have to fix it soon because the Rosebud Coalmine which had recently opened up, relied upon it to bring the teams across that hauled the coal from the mine to the railroad. He suggested that I cross the river and visit the mine, to find out if I could, when the ferry would be repaired.

It was too late to go that day, so I stayed in camp hoping that the river would go down some before morning, it didn't, but I set out anyway. I headed across the river on horseback. My horse was small but it could sure swim, and I hung on for dear life. We were being swept downstream, and I was afraid the horse would be played out before we reached the other side. It was quite a struggle, and there were times when I thought we wouldn't make it. When we finally did, my horse had had all it could take. I don't believe I would have started the swim if I had realized the width of the river, and the strength of the current. I had started about a quarter of a mile upstream, thinking this would bring me out at the landing, but we were over half a mile downstream from the landing before we reached the other side.

I rode up to the mine, the boss was just coming out and he stopped in astonishment.

"Just where in the world did you come from?" he asked. I told him all my troubles, but he was still doubtful that I had swum the river, until he felt my clothes and found I was soaking wet. He told me that the men were away downstream trying to salvage the ferry from where it had lodged in the bush. They had taken teams, and were going to try and haul it back upstream to where it had broken loose. He advised me to camp where I was until they had repaired it.

He had an old boat down by the river in the bush, and he offered to take me back across the river in it. I was sure thankful, as I wasn't anxious to swim on my horse again. The boat had been out of the river for some time and was pretty leaky, so I was kept busy bailing all the way across. My horse managed to swim by itself without too much trouble. We dragged the boat back upstream so that he could have a longer run at the landing on the other side. I helped him push off, and watched anxiously as he bailed and rowed across the river.

I rode back down the river to our camp, where I found everything in order. The stock seemed contented to stay put, so there was little to do but explore the valley. Riding round the valley it seemed we were in a different world, it was hard to believe that this country was part of Alberta, it was most different.

The valley was a mile wide and four hundred feet deep. The cliffs were bare and weathered showing different coloured layers of rock. Little did we dream that there were dinosaur bones buried there. There was hardly a sign of life except for our stock, grey grass-snakes, and grey lizards sunning themselves in the dirt. The only time we could see the lizards, was when they blinked their eyes. There were not many ground squirrels in those days, for there were plenty of bull snakes to feed on them. Bull snakes grew so big; I've seen one that was eight feet long, and as thick as a man's arm.

13

We came across tall hoodoos, I could see one in the distance and on the top were about a dozen big, black birds with red heads and necks, sunning themselves. I thought, who in the world keeps turkeys around here? When I got closer, I realized they were turkey vultures, and the only ones I have seen in Alberta. I watched them for a long time, then I took a shot at them, they flew up high into the sky, and I never saw them again.

It was six or seven days before the ferryman came and said he would be able to take us over the river the next day. We were down at the ferry bright and early the next morning. Deciding to take the horses over first, we drove them onto the ferry, they promptly jumped off the other end, and swam across the river.

Before we drove the cows on, we tied a rope across the opposite end of the ferry. That didn't work, they just crowded to one end which tipped the ferry up, dumping them in the river in a heap. We watched them anxiously as they swam across the river, but they all made it to shore. Wills and I crossed on the ferry with the wagon. Later we noticed that one two-year old heifer had broken one front leg below the knee, I sold this to the mine for $15 and the cook butchered it.

Our next problem was to get out of the valley. The only trail was straight up a hog's back of a hill; the mine boss came to our rescue, by sending a man and team to double up on our outfit. Even so we had a difficult time to get our wagon up to the top bench, and without their help we couldn't have made it.

Once on top we drifted north and had no trouble until we got to the Imperial Ranch, this was Burn's outfit, and quite a spread. I believe they had at least 3,000 cows, and 90 bulls in the herd. There were also farmers through here, and somehow we lost two yearling steers. I spent two days looking for them but there wasn't a sign of them anywhere. I asked several farmers but they hadn't seen them, so I gave up looking. Two years later they turned up in the Calgary stockyards.

After over a month on the trail we reached the lake. I left Wills to keep smudges going as the mosquitoes were quite bad. A smudge is a fire of smoke to discourage insects. I then went back by train to the 'Hat' to bring the rest of the outfit and the milk cows.

CHAPTER THREE

Doren Lee and Red Deer Lake

My move to the lake proved to be a good one, at least we were able to grow feed and grain for the stock. During the time I lived at Red Deer Lake, I was Secretary of the local School Board, and a Councillor for our Municipal District. Here I learnt a thing or two about building roads. There was a Provincial road between Wetaskiwin and Ferintosh going through a slough which was miles long. We used to avoid this slough by going over a farmer's land, but in time he objected to this, and insisted that we fix the road.

I decided that the best thing to do was to drain it. So we got permission to dig a ditch a spade's width, and drain the water out. Next I went to our M.L.A.*in Camrose, George P. Smith, and asked him to get us $800 to fix the road, which he did. We brought slips of dirt, and pushed them into the hole with a Fresno pulled by a tractor, just exactly as a caterpillar tractor does today.

After we'd fixed the road across the slough, it had cost about $600, so I went down the road quite a ways, and spent $200 to fill the next slough hole. When we put in the pay sheets, they wouldn't pay the $200, as they said the $800 had been allocated for the first slough hole, and that's where it had to be spent. Well I learned a lesson right there!

At home we had a cabinet of about fifty butterflies that Mother's uncle had collected in India, I guess this gave me the idea of making a collection of Alberta butterflies. Our hired man was a happy-go-lucky Scotsman named Jack Mackintosh, he was breaking land and picking roots for Dad; he would work out in the rain in overalls but barefoot and without a hat. We shared a room over the kitchen, and he and I collected butterflies. We collected eggs, caterpillars, and cocoons and looked after them at night after work, until they emerged into butterflies, they were scattered in different boxes all over our room. We had a good collection, and when I left the district I gave it to the school.

When war came in 1918, Percy Wills and Jack Mackintosh decided to join up. I took them to Bashaw to the recruiting office, and while talking to the recruiting officer, I told him I had half a mind to join up myself.

"They wouldn't take you with that gammy leg," he told me.

"I was thinking of the cavalry, I wasn't going to walk!" I said. He told me I had enough to do looking after all my cows, and he was right, for I had

---

*Member of the Legislative Assembly.

practically no help after Percy and Jack left, and I worked all day and all night at times.

Dr. J. R. McLeod the first M.L.A. for Ferintosh, was our physician and our druggist. I was Councillor for the district which comprised a township and a half that was fully settled up. When the Influenza epidemic hit the district, I was sworn in by Dr. McLeod to be his assistant. I hauled feed for my own stock, and went around visiting people who were sick, giving them medicine from Dr. McLeod, and arranging for someone to come in and feed their stock and look after them. I used my car to get about and I was on the go all the time.

One day someone noticed that there was no smoke from the house on the hill where a bachelor lived alone, so I went up to investigate. I found him dead, and informed his parents who came and looked after everything. He was the only one that died in our district. We all wore masks, but eventually I caught it. It hit so suddenly, two brothers who lived three or four miles away, promised to come and haul feed for my stock when they heard I was ill, but before they could come they were taken ill themselves, and I had to struggle on alone.

I had built a frame house on my place and started up on my own, then I married a girl named Louise Barr, who was born in Wisconsin, and came to Alberta with her mother, sister and stepfather, when she was two or three years old. Louise was raised on a farm and she was a wonderful worker, she could harness and hook up a four horse team just as good as any man. Out in the field with four horses, she'd work all day pitching bundles or anything. She and her sister came home at night and milked five or six cows, and they put down enough bacon, hams, and sausages to last a whole year.

I grew feed and grain for the stock, and everything went well until the severe winter of 1919-1920. Winter moved in with a bang, the first week of October. I had quite a big herd and was doubtful if I had enough feed for the winter. Wild hay was getting scarce, so was pasture on C.P.R. land, as farmers were moving in and buying it up.

More than half the farmers, including one who lived ten miles up the lake from me, didn't get threshed at all, so I bought oat bundles from him for 25¢ each. The snow got deep and I had to dig them out, this meant digging oat bundles all day and hauling at night. The lake was good for sleighing which was the only consolation. This turned out to be a record, hard winter. We lost a lot of cattle, they just perished with the continuous cold.

Cows were hard to sell, and even if you could sell them, they only brought $35-$40. That winter Burns, the Packers and Ranchers had a contract to supply Belgium with five million dollars worth of breeding stock, to restock their herds after the war. We weren't being asked to give them to Belgium, they were paying good money for them, and this would have relieved some of the ranchers of their surplus stock.

Unfortunately the Government of Alberta put an embargo on she stock going out of the Province, in order not to deplete the breeding stock of Alberta. Ted Gardner, who was buying for Burns, had only spent $800,000 when the embargo was enforced, and as he couldn't get any more cows in Alberta, he went to Kansas to fill the contract.

According to a rough census taken by the Royal Canadian Mounted Police the next spring, about a million dollars worth of breeding cows died that winter of cold and starvation. These cows could have been shipped to Belgium, leaving enough feed for those that were left, I lost fifty head of cows myself.

By now I had been at the lake for seven years, and on the whole had done fairly well with my cattle, and hated to leave, but to move seemed the only thing to do.

I was discussing the question of the rancher's shortage of pasture with Burn's brother-in-law, Charlie Duggan, of Duggan, Hills and Campbell. They were in the livestock commission business in Edmonton, and they told me that ranchers from all over Alberta were shipping cattle to the Peace River country. They themselves were already trying this out, having in the previous fall, shipped a hundred head of cows into the Battle River country, which was about a hundred miles north of the town of Peace River Crossing. They had applied for a lease, though hadn't got it as yet. They were not happy about the way things were being looked after, and suggested that I put my cows in with theirs and run the entire outfit as a company. I knew this outfit fairly well, as I was shipping stock to them in Edmonton.

I had stock in the yards, and instead of hanging around I decided to go up to town, which at that time was five miles away. There was no means of transport at that time of day, so I walked. As I came closer to town, I noticed a little store and post office, so I went in looking for something to drink. What a surprise I had when I got inside, there was Percy Wills!

He had been wounded in the war and sent back to Canada, but not before he had married a Welsh girl. His wife was a fine little woman though as hard to understand as Wills for she spoke the same lingo. We talked for hours about all the things that had happened to us since we parted. I also told him of my intention of moving again if I could find anything suitable, and suggested that he might like to come along.

"Not likely!" he said, ' I helped you move once, that was more than enough for me!"

I never saw Wills again after I left him that night, the next time I called in he had sold out and moved. It was night-time before I finally made the hotel. How fast things change, those stockyards are swallowed up by the city today!

I decided that I would go up to the Peace River country and take a look around. I went north with Vick Campbell, who was going to see how their outfit was getting along. It was May when we set out from Peace River, then called Peace River Crossing, on horseback.

We followed an old Indian wagon trail made by the elk and bison hunters, which wandered around from one camping place to another; a lake where they could hunt ducks or geese, or a prairie where there was feed for their horses. It was very rough, not cut out much, and there were muskegs where we had to dismount and lead our horses.

It was about ninety miles and we rode right through in one day. Vick was a big man and not used to riding a horse, he was all in when we came to his foreman's place at Notikewin. We had supper, and then rolled in our blankets and slept on the floor for the night. In the morning Vick was so stiff he couldn't move.

I spent a week with Vick and his foreman riding around looking for their hundred head of cattle. It was all windfall, with a patch of grass here and

17

another patch of grass a mile away, the cows were scattered all over the wind-fall, we never did find all of them. They had put out forty head of horses too, and they were never seen again, no-one knew where they went. I thought to myself, this is no place to try and raise cows.

However, I was talking to one of the natives and he told me about Keg River Prairie, he said there was plenty of open country there, and no-one in the cattle business.

Duggan, Hills, and Campbell held their outfit down in Battle River for about three years, then they had to quit. After two years their application for a lease was turned down by the Government, as the surveyors reported that the land was suitable for farming, how right they were! Duggan, Hills, and Campbell, shipped out a few more head than they brought in, but the entire endeavour was a huge failure as the cattle shipped out were worth nothing.

I rode back to Peace River thinking I would maybe try my luck at Keg River. While there, I ran into A. J. Bryson and Vern McLean, ranchers from the Cypress Hills, they had moved their stock to the Ft. St. John country where they had leased a township on Whisky Creek. They suggested that I go up there with them, but I decided against it.

I bought a horse from Jack Mckinnon the liveryman, then I waited for the boat, the D. A. Thomas, to go downstream to Keg River Landing. There was no road then from Battle River to Keg River, only a blazed packtrail, this was about a hundred miles long, and you had to have a pack outfit and know the trail, which was hard to find in places, that was why I hung around in Peace River waiting for the boat.

While waiting for the boat I talked to several cattlemen who had shipped cattle in from the south, they were not impressed with the country. They had all moved in too late in the year to find adequate feed, so had put their stock out in farmer's straw piles around Fairview and Waterhole, where they had to lick snow for water. This is no way to raise stock in the north, it is too bleak and cold. I was still determined to see the Keg River country, and when the D. A. Thomas was loaded for the trip downriver, I took my horse on board and went downstream with it.

Keg River Landing was on the north bank of the Peace River, and across the river from Carcajou Point, about two hundred miles downstream from Peace River Crossing. We arrived at the landing the following morning. There were only two warehouses there belonging to the Hudson's Bay Company and Revillon Freres. I left right away for the Keg River Prairie, as I had been told that it was about forty miles inland.

There was a steep hill at the landing, and another big hill at Keg River Crossing, otherwise the country was fairly flat. The trail went through sloughs and muskegs for thirty miles before it hit Keg River Prairie. It was tough going but I made it before dark and found a trapper who was willing to feed me and bed me down.

The trapper was Dick Hutchings, a war veteran, who worked on the Government survey in the summer. They were surveying the fifth meridian in the north at that time and made Keg River their winter headquarters, survey-ing the prairie at the same time. Dick was wintering the packhorses until C. P. Hotchkiss, the Dominion Land Surveyor came back to continue working.

The natives owned a herd of horses that they used to pack their belongings into the bush in the fall, when they went to their traplines. In the spring they burnt off the prairie, this didn't harm the soil but cleared all the rank grass, and killed off all the small poplars that had grown up during the previous summer. In this way the prairie was preserved, and the poplars kept under control. As time went on of course, the Government installed the Forestry Service and burning grass was prohibited, consequently the poplars took over and the prairie started to diminish. Today it costs a farmer much time and plenty of money to clear the land of poplar bush before he can break it up and put in a crop.

Dick Hutchings informed me that hay was waist high by August, and hundreds of acres of it, he offered to come with me and we rode around all day looking things over. I camped with him again that night satisfied with what I had seen.

Back in Edmonton, I met J. A. Hills and told him of what I had seen and done. Hills said, they were not satisfied with their ranching in Battle River, especially as there were so many flies in the summer. Dick had not mentioned flies! It was early in the season with only the odd mosquito out. I told myself there were flies all over. Hills told me also that he had been up to Grande Prairie to look around, and he figured it was a better location for stock, he advised me to take a look there also before I made any decisions.

I left the next day and finding a neighbour Cecil Dore on the same quest we joined forces. The returning veterans were being outfitted by the Veteran's Land Act to go farming. They all seemed to be going towards Pouce Coupé, so we decided to head that way, in a Model T Ford that we had hired.

We got as far as Saskatoon Lake, where we saw that many of the Veterans with their oufits, had camped along the lake the previous night, turning their teams loose to graze. When we arrived, they had them collected up and there were some arguments going on. They had only owned their horses for a day or so, and didn't know them any too well. They were going by the bill of sales that they had.

"My bill of sale says, 'Bay gelding, with white spot on forehead, no brand, about six years old.' and that's what I've got," one fellow would say.

"My bill of sale says the same," the other fellow would reply. And so it went!

We left them to it, and continued on towards Pouce Coupé, we didn't get very far. There was only a wagon trail, no road, just mud, and we had to stay in the wagon tracks as there was windfall timber on both sides. We had had enough of this and as soon as we found a place where we could turn round we went back to Grande Prairie. Most of the men at Saskatoon Lake were still there, we passed one man dragging a mowing machine through the mud behind his wagon, he had a lot to learn! However, many of them made good.

Dore and I parted in Edmonton, and I went on home to tell Louise about my travels. We agreed to give Keg River a try. Farmers couldn't bother us there for it was over two hundred miles to the nearest town, and there was no market for their produce.

CHAPTER FOUR

Extremely Dangerous and

Badly Constructed

While I was collecting my haying outfit together, an old ranch hand came along looking for a job, I hired him, and a useful man he was. With the mowers and rakes, I took twenty head of work horses, two wagons, and a camp outfit loaded in a democrat. We loaded them onto a car of Settler's Effects at Ferintosh on the Grand Trunk Pacific Railway, this had good connections with the Edmonton, Dunvegan and British Columbia Railway which was the railroad from Edmonton to Judah.

Judah was way up on the hill about twelve miles out of Peace River, and as far as we could go on the train at that time. There was a track to Peace River, but it kept slipping down the hill, and every so often they drove pilings in to try and hold it. When we arrived, we put our wagons together and started hauling everything down the hill to the boat landing. It took all day to make one trip up and down that hill. A haying machine is hard to pack, it's light but bulky. The horses were good, they worked from early in the morning until late at night, and it took several trips to get everything down.

The hill was steep, but we rough-locked the wheels, and had no incidents, except that we were persecuted by flies. When we got to the boatlanding, we had to unload, and when the boat came in we had to load everything onto it, then when we reached Carcajou, it was all to unload again, altogether an exhausting task for men and horses.

We had a four horse team on each of the two wagons, but we soon found out that this wasn't enough horse power. The wagons sank up to their axles in mud, and we still had thirty miles to go! In addition to this, we were being eaten alive by mosquitoes, bulldog flies, and no-see-ums, which seriously tortured the workhorses. If you have never experienced these flies, it's impossible to imagine what they are like. The bulldog flies used to be so bad, that if we went over a hole with water in it, the horses would try and flop down in the mud to escape from them. When they stirred up the mud it smelled horrible! I remembered what Hills had said about flies, and began to wonder, this state of affairs didn't look any too good for cattle.

We kept going somehow, and made the prairie on the second day. However, this was only the first trip, it took two or more before we finished hauling all the haying machinery to Keg River. We put the machinery together and started haying right there. Some of the natives came round and I hired those I needed for a dollar a day in grub. The two trading posts, the

21

Hudson's Bay and Revillon Freres, were closed during the summer. They were two or three miles from my camp, but in any case, they didn't want to see an Indian unless he had fur to trade.

The prospects looked good, the hay was so tall, that when a man and a team went down the prairie, you could see nothing but his head and the horses ears. There were only a few other people haying, freighters, and natives who needed hay for their horses. I stayed with the outfit for a couple of weeks to see that things were running smoothly, then left for home.

I had to wait about a day before the boat came along, which gave me plenty of time to think and wonder about those flies. It had cost me $700, not to mention the labour involved, to move the haying outfit and start haying, I really had no choice but to go ahead.

As I was waiting for the boat, an old Indian came across the river from Carcajou Point in a dugout canoe, he tried to tell me to come across the river, as the boat always stopped there. He couldn't speak English, and I couldn't speak Cree, but we managed to communicate. I pointed to my horse and made him to understand that I had to keep the smudge going, otherwise he would be eaten alive by flies. We chewed the rag for a time and then he left.

I found out later that he was Xavier Sowan, and I got to know him quite well. He had a cabin, but lived in a teepee in his front yard. I stayed with him quite often while waiting for the boat, he and his wife were sure a good hearted couple. Xavier at that time was still hunting with a bow and arrow. The bow was made of birch about five feet high with a little bit of a curve but not much. The string was made of babiche, thin strips of rawhide cut straight and rolled while wet.

The arrows were about as thick as a pencil, two feet long and made out of chokecherry wood, the shaft and head all in one. The arrow heads were sharp and very brittle, and they took a long time to make. The old man would sit outside the teepee in front of the fire making arrows. He would char the point in the fire and rub off the charcoal, hardening them and sharpening them. Sometimes he split the end of the arrow and bound feathers in between, otherwise he would just bind the feathers at the side of the shaft.

He had two or three sizes of arrows suitable for muskrats and beaver; for bigger game he used a rifle. If he shot a beaver or a rat, and it sank under the water, he retrieved it with an eagle's foot attached to a pole. The foot was as big as a man's hand, and he'd stick the claws into the animal, give the pole a bit of a twist and bring it up.

It was not long after Sowan left that the boat came up the river, and it was a good thing I had a smudge going so that they could see me, as they hadn't intended to stop at the landing.

When I got home I started rounding up my cattle, they were supposed to be in my pasture, though feed being scarce they had crawled through the fence and were scattered all over the country. I ordered cars to load out from Dorenlee. We had two sons by now, Louis who was born in 1918, and Arthur who was born in 1919. My folks helped me to haul my furniture, a dozen crated chickens, five milk cows, and later my saddle horse, to be shipped as Settler's Effects, which were entitled to a cheaper freight rate. All this time my brother-in-law Albert Pierson was helping me with my cows, and I couldn't have managed without him.

22

In Edmonton every hoof had to be unloaded, fed and watered, as it was supposed to be at every divisional, which is the end of the run for the train crews. While there I sorted out all the calves and sold them to help me to carry on. Cows were worth nothing, especially mine as they were in such poor condition. While loading the cattle in the Edmonton yards, the train conductor asked me where I was shipping them to. I told him I was shipping them to Peace River Crossing, and then two hundred miles further north.

"Boy!" he said, ,'Sell them here and now, I have hauled trainloads of cattle to the Peace River country this past year, it's just a graveyard for cows!" This wasn't very encouraging, but it was too late now to take his advice. I rode in the caboose with the conductor, and I asked him what the initials E.D. & B.C. stood for.

"Extremely Dangerous and Badly Constructed," he informed me, and believe me he wasn't joking!

The railroad didn't have a solid bed for it was built over muskegs, also the steel was too light. A section crew was based every eight or nine miles to fix the track. The railbed would sink under the tracks and the crew would haul gravel in a wheelbarrow, lift the ties, and shove it underneath. Looking at the rails from the observation car at the back of the train, it was hard to understand how the train stayed on the track at all for the rails were all twisted and warped. Looking back after going round a bend, you could see the track swing back out of place after the train had pulled it in. In some places the track was under water. It used to take us three days to get to Peace River, they'd shove the train into a siding while they fixed the track, we never knew when we would arrive.

Not far out of Westlock the train came to a halt, and the conductor went forward to investigate. He came back to say they had run over a cow and did I think it was mine? I told him it might be if he hadn't fastened the doors properly, but in any case, I didn't think we were going fast enough to run over a cow! Before we got going again an old woman came along to see the conductor, and find out what he was going to do about killing her cow! We got moving again and didn't stop until we reached Smith, which was the next divisional.

At Smith, the conductor ordered me to unload my cattle and feed and water them as it was the rule for this to be done at all divisionals. I told him I had no intention of doing so as there was no feed to be had, and the corrals were too poor to hold the cattle, also there was no water, except the river.

In Edmonton I had agreed to look after some cows bought by the Government under the Cow Bill Act, consigned to Peace River. I told the conductor I couldn't mix two different shipments of cattle in one corral. I also told him that if he didn't pull me out right away, I would relinquish my charge of looking after the Government cows and he could take over. He said he would see the agent, and see what he could do. The next thing I knew, the engine came along, hooked onto our cars, and I hightailed it to the caboose.

During the night, on the way to McLennan we got a hot-axle box on one of the freight cars, it took the crew hours to fix. I stayed in the caboose, when the conductor went forward he left the door of the caboose open behind him, so when he came back the caboose was full of mosquitoes. The conductor and the brakeman were sure mad! They had been fighting flies half the night, and to come back to a caboose full of them was just too much. I reminded the conductor that it was he that had left the door open, and I'd presumed he wanted it that way, though if it had been me I would have closed it after me.

Eventually we reached McLennan, the next divisional, where they shunted the stock cars down to the corrals. I went straight to the agent who insisted that I must feed and water the stock. There were good corrals this time with several different pens, but no feed and no water. I tried to explain this to the agent, but he said if I couldn't feed them, I could take them down to the lake, half a mile away and water them.

In turn I pointed out to him that it was only fifty miles to Peace River, and I refused to unload the cattle until we got there. He refused to pull me out, so I asked him for two telegraph forms and wrote one to the Superintendent in Edmonton, and one to the Government agent who had asked me to look after their cows. I pushed them across to him and asked him to send them.

"What's this?" he asked.

I told him I intended to find out why I couldn't get to Peace River without unloading. He told me to hold them until he could see what he could do. I agreed, and told him I would be at the lunch counter in the station building. I hadn't eaten for over a day, and I was getting hungry. The train crew cook their meals in the caboose, but never offered so much as a drink of tea to anybody.

After I left the agent, I ran into Neil Sutherland who was the Government agent from Peace River, and he'd come to take charge of the cows. I told him my troubles and he agreed that I shouldn't let them kid me into unloading the cattle. He went off to see the agent himself, and I ordered breakfast. When it came, I was just about to eat it, when Neil rushed in,

"Frank," he yelled, "If you're coming to Peace River, come now!"

I beat it, leaving my breakfast on the table, uneaten and unpaid for! Our stock cars were hooked on, and we only just managed to climb on the caboose as the train pulled out. I asked Neil what had happened. He said he told the agent who he was, and the agent said he would have the cars ready to leave right away, and that was all.

When we got to the end of steel we unloaded my cows first. After collecting them we took them to Peace River, crossed the railway bridge to where the golf course is now, and turned them loose. There was plenty of water in the little slough holes, and it was a great relief to them as they had been in the cars for three days. I put my milk cows in McKinnon's yard, and made arrangements with him to haul my furniture and chickens, if there were any still alive, to the boat. Then at last I had time to go and find something to eat. This was my second day without eating.

I stopped at Nagle's Grill and ate everything in sight, then I headed for the Royal Hotel to see how Louise and the boys were making out. The Royal Hotel was a good hotel, it even had a bathroom, however, if you wanted water you had to take a pail down to the river for it! Later the Royal was moved into town and called the Victory.

I talked to some natives and old-timers about the feasibility of taking the cattle overland to Keg River. They all advised me against this as they considered it was too late in the season. Also, the natives said there was only a packtrail through the bush from Notikewin to Keg River, and if it snowed I would really be up against it. The cattle were in such poor condition, I knew they couldn't stand any more hardship, so I decided to take their advice.

Meanwhile I was herding my cows up on the hills in the daytime, they were no trouble at all, and started to fill out on the plentiful pasture. To save night herding, I made arrangements with Mr. H. A. George, a grand old-timer who was living on his homestead at the top of the hill, to put the cows in his fenced pasture at night.

I went to make enquiries about taking my cows to Keg River landing on the boat. The boat was on its last trip according to their schedule, though it returned that night, and in the morning the captain agreed to take me on condition that I loaded that night and paid the cost of the trip — one thousand dollars, in cash. I drew the money out of the bank which almost cleaned me out of cash, and told the captain I would have the cattle there by sundown.

I managed to find time to go and inform Louise of my plans, and asked her to go down and get on board as soon as possible. I had the cows down at the landing just after dark, helped by McKinnon's hired man. I had also asked McKinnon to have my milk cows down at the landing by dark, tied up somewhere close, as I intended to lead them on the boat first to entice the others on. When I saw the boat, I began to doubt that we would ever get them on board.

The boat was brilliantly lit with electric lights, and the engines were turning. The boat had a flat deck just about five feet above the water, and there was a door at each side for loading. The captain figured that it would be best to load them from the front as the side doors were big and they might see each other milling around and not go on.

We started to load them from the front, they had to pass down a narrow passageway on the right of the engines which were at the back of the boat. We hardly had five minutes trouble, they went on like a bunch of people used to getting on a boat. One or two went back and got into a chicken run, I remember riding over chicken wire, and a chicken house, but we got them all on safely.

We pulled out right away and the next night just at dark, we hit Keg River Landing. We just opened the doors and let them go, I knew they would just go up the hill and find something to eat, there was nowhere else to go. We were sure in luck at the landing, August LaFleur was there with his team. August had come down for some flour he had ordered from Peace River. He had expected me to be on the last boat, and knowing I would have no transportation, he had caught a team of mine and brought it along, his wife driving it.

August was a small good-hearted French-Canadian half breed, he was lightly built with a thin face, his wife, unlike most of the native women, was tall and slim. We camped in one of the warehouses for the night, and during the night two feet of snow fell. It was still snowing in the morning when we loaded the wagons with essentials and pulled out. It was cold and the snow was heavy and wet, making it tough travelling. We only had small pieces of tarp to keep us dry and everything got soaked.

We picked up the cows about two miles along the trail, and it was noon before it quit snowing. We camped for the night at Keg River Crossing about twelve miles from the landing, this was a good camping place with thick spruce which is good in the winter for camping, as there is no snow underneath.

I took the cows on about four miles, and left them in a slough for the night. The next morning the going was still tough with mud and snow, but the snow wasn't quite as deep. We hoped to make it home that day but first one of August's horses played out, and then one of mine quit. My horses were so thin, the boys had worked them hard at haying, and of course they had no oats. We had no choice but to leave one wagon to pick up another time, and make a team out of the horses that were still able to work, leading our played out horses.

About ten miles from home we stopped at a cabin belonging to a native called Blackbird. Old Blackbird was a short, wiry, shrivelled up French-Canadian half-breed, who couldn't speak English, but August was able to translate for us. They sure made us welcome, they had made hay so we were able to feed our horses, Mrs. Blackbird made us dinner, and we were all glad to thaw out.

As we sat down to dinner August fell over backwards in a faint, the cold and wet having got the better of him. I jumped up and beat it out to the wagon, got a bottle of brandy out of my grip, and poured some into him. That straightened him up alright! Old Blackbird said that he was sick too, but I told August to tell him to go to bed, and he would soon feel better.

I left the cows in the sloughs where they were feeding on the long slough grass, the snow being soft, they were able to push it away easily. We arrived home by dark. The boys I had left haying had put up two small barns, so I had a place to put my two played out horses. My chickens were all alive, even though they had been penned up for nearly two weeks.

Dick Hutchings had loaned me his cabin for the summer as he had been working on the survey, it was made of logs and was twenty-four feet, by fifteen feet. It stood at the edge of a spruce grove, next to the prairie and was all we needed for the time being.

Next morning, looking out upon the cold prairie, with the cows twenty-five miles away and as thin as they could get, I wondered where I'd gone wrong. I thought to myself, that I ought to have taken the train conductor's advice in Edmonton, it seemed now to have been perfect. However, here we were and here we would have to stay, at least for a few years until the price of cattle improved, then we could pull out. That was over fifty years ago and I'm still here!

Train at Peace River 1916. Photo Glenbow-Alberta Institute.

Mr. Brick's farm — Peace River — 1907. Photo Archives of British Columbia.

S.S. D. A. Thomas in the 1920s. Photo Peace River Centennial Museum.

Railroad track tipped by slide on hill, east of Peace River 1916. Photo Glenbow-Alberta Institute.

CHAPTER FIVE

First Winter at Keg River

The next morning I went down to the village; seeing smoke at the Hudson's Bay post I called in. The manager, Joe Kemp, was back for the winter. He told me about Sam Baptiste Wanuch who agreed to help me bring in the cows. Sam came on his saddle horse, and we found the cattle, gathered them up, and started for home. We camped at Blackbirds that night leaving the cattle feeding along the creek. In the morning they seemed to be quite happy with their new grazing ground so Sam and I cut out the milk cows, which I took home, leaving the rest to graze.

When I got home I found Dick Hutchings there, he said we could keep the cabin for the winter, as he was going to look after the surveyor's horses at Buffalo Prairie, south of Ft. Vermilion. It was a great help to me to have the cabin, and I heartily appreciated it. Dick gave me permission to build on a room to make it large enough for us. The weather turned mild, and most of the snow melted, Dick was in no hurry to leave so he stayed to help us for a few days. We had our cabin extension up in three days, though without chinking or windows. I had two windows at the landing with the rest of our goods. I didn't intend to go back for them until the mud and the snow had frozen hard enough to use the two sleighs I had at the river.

While Dick had been busy getting logs out of the bush, I had gone to check on the hay that the boys had put up. Taking advice from August La Fleur who told me I would need plenty, as it is late before the grass grows again, I decided to cut some more hay. The peavine was still easy to cut as the snow had not packed it down as much as the tall grass, although it was badly frozen, it would be better than nothing.

Most of the trappers had pulled out or were getting ready to go, but Joe Kemp told me his brother Kid Kemp would probably work for me. Kid agreed, so I went out to look for my horses. I found them all but one bay mare. I didn't find this mare until the next spring, a trapper saw her at the mouth of the Battle River, she had gone back to the Peace, followed it up, making over a hundred miles. Presumably she was making for her old home, she had more brains than I.

The horses were very thin, but I gave Kid the best team I could muster, and left him to see what he could do. He mowed for two days and then gave it up, it was impossible to mow any more as the mower slipped over the top of the hay. However, we collected what he had already cut, raked it, tied it into bunches and later we hauled about twenty loads.

After we finished the cabin extension, we built a big shed for the cattle, while working on this it turned cold and snowed again, so after checking on the cows which were still rustling in the snow, we fetched the rest of our things from the landing, bringing them back in sleighs.

Soon after this I collected up the cows, counted them and brought them home. We found that we had a small branded steer which wasn't mine, and one of my cows was missing. I inquired and found out that the few cattle which the natives owned and kept on the prairie, weren't branded. During the winter I wrote to Jack McKinnon, and found out that this steer belonged to A. Brown and Carmine, ranchers from High River, and my cow was on C. C. Northay's homestead not far from where I had held the cattle on the hills, outside Peace River town.

I wrote to A. Brown and Carmine and told them what had happened, in their reply they told me that they had shipped three hundred head of cattle to the Peace River country, and this was, as far as they knew, the only one left. They had lost all the rest, including nine or ten bulls that were seized by a liveryman who had wintered them in his yard. I sent them $35 for their steer, and they said that my cheque was the only money they had got back out of the entire herd!

Meanwhile winter set in with a vengeance. The waterholes in the creek all froze up, so I had to break ice to water the cows. I used a four horse team to haul hay for them from the stacks which were a mile away. The snow got to be quite deep, and to make matters worse there was a continuous wind that kept the trail drifted, it was a tough job, and there was no escape, every morning I had to get out there and haul hay. I had some adjacent buildings, a small barn I used for my three bulls, and another one for horses and milk cows. I still had two cows milking, and I managed to get them up in their milk again so we had plenty of milk to make butter and cheese, though we were at a disadvantage not having a cream separator. I had brought a big churn with me, and a one-horse Fairbanks engine to run it, this did double duty running the washing machine.

A man called Pete Lizotte came in from Ft. Vermilion intending to work as an interpreter for Revillons, instead he came to work for me, and he worked for me on and off for quite a number of years, he was a good worker.

The cattle didn't come through the winter as well as I expected considering the amount of hay they ate, and one of them got drowned in a waterhole. Keeping the waterholes open was a nightmare, we had to keep chopping new holes. The ice was so thick it would freeze to the bottom of the river, then the water had to find a new outlet, and it would flood all over the ice and freeze again. The cow must have slipped while drinking, and was unable to get a foothold, or her head out of the water. The winter had been cold and tough, and I didn't have enough hay to see me through. There was no weight to the hay here, it took over 600 cu. ft. to make a ton, whereas in southern Alberta it took 350-380 cu. ft., and in the Red Deer Lake area it took about 450 cu. ft. to make a ton. I discovered this in later years when I started to bale hay. Fortunately August La Fleur had a haystack that he had put up for the surveyors, as they didn't need it, I was able to buy it which was a help.

My horses weren't doing as well as they should, I had no oats, and there were none to be had. I had three or four horses wintering in some sloughs upriver from home. Towards spring I went to see how they were making out, I found them as thin as they could get, so took them home. I put two of them in the barn, they had no appetite even though I gave them the best hay I had. They picked it over, and died in a short time. Joe Kemp told me that all horses brought in from outside died of the same complaint, though the Indian cayuses seemed to be immune from it.

I wrote to my brother-in-law Dr. Robert Boyd, Grace's husband who was a vet, asking his advice. At that time we received mail once a month, and none in November and April, so it was months before I received a reply, and by this time two more horses had died. My brother-in-law told me that they had swamp fever, and sent me some medicine to try on them. Altogether I lost seventeen horses with swamp fever. I found out later that all the horses shipped in from outside to Ft. Vermilion died of swamp fever.

When the Manning district, then called the Battle River District, was being settled by farmers from Saskatchewan in 1929 and 1930, they brought in some of the finest horses you could wish to see. In a year or two they were all dead. Swamp fever is carried by some mosquitoes, but at this time we had no idea how it was carried, we only knew it was a big disaster, and many farmers went broke because of it.

In April and May the cows started to calve, then my troubles really started. Many cows appeared to be dry, they didn't spring, had no milk, went sick, stopped grazing, and lay down and died. After I lost two or three, I knew that something was really wrong.

The next cow that died, I opened up and found a fully developed calf that had been dead about a week or so. It would have been impossible to get this calf from behind, or even to have cut it up and removed it, because the cow was so contracted. The next cow that went sick, I tried caesarian section. I performed caesarian sections on five cows, just as soon as I saw they were sick, I had no disinfectant except Creolin, and only string to sew them up, so I saved the calves but lost the cows. The calves had to be hand-fed, and this took all the milk we had, so I had to give this up. Altogether I lost thirty cows.

I sent samples of the hay out to The University of Alberta, thinking maybe weed seeds in the local hay had caused the sickness, but no-one had ever heard of it before. I have experienced it on several occasions since that first winter.

I asked Joe Kemp if he knew anything about the trouble I was having with my cows, as the native cattle seemed to be alright. He said that the natives lose cattle all the time, and if you ask them what was the matter with their cow, they just shrug and say, .

"Oh she died, Lots of dog feed!"
I hauled the last hay home for the bulls and the milk cows. I was down to three horses by now, so it was a good job that I had no need of them, though small comfort.

The snow had gone, the ice had melted in the river, and the mosquitoes were out in droves. They kept the cattle on the run day and night. I built smudges for them later, but at first I thought they could manage without them. The windows and door of the cabin weren't screened, so we had to have smudges going all the time, to obtain some relief from those flies.

Then calamity struck again. I went home one morning after seeing to the ninety or so cows I had left, to find Pete with bad news.

"We've lost two of the bulls, I don't know how they got out, the fence

31

isn't broken anywhere, and the gate hasn't been left open." We went to look for them, the only tracks that we could find led down to the river. The river has steep mud banks, and is all bends and deep water during the spring runoff. We came to a log jam and crossed the river, there we found one bull jammed in the logs, dead. On looking further we found the other bull under the logs, also dead. We concluded that they were either fighting at the edge of the river and fell in, or the logs came loose upstream and swept them to their death.

These animals were pure-bred Hereford bulls that had cost me $800 each, one of them was a grandson of the famous Fairfax Perfection. This was a big blow to me on top of everything else. I was left with only one bull, it looked as if he would have to work overtime!

Most of the trappers had returned with their families from their traplines and were settling down in their teepees for the summer. Some of them came to my place wanting to trade for flour, lard, etc., I refused to trade for fur, but told them that if they would make hay for me, I would pay them in groceries, cheaper than at the trading posts.

Here I was facing the haying season with no horses. The natives didn't have enough cayuses big enough to make hay to sell me, so I decided to go south to see what I could find. Louise said that she had had enough of travelling on the journey in, the milk cows had freshened and needed to be milked, I had planted a garden, and this needed looking after, so she stayed at home and I headed south.

CHAPTER SIX

Horses Down Jasper Avenue

Louise never went to school, but her mother taught her to speak, read and write, English, German, Norwegian and Swedish. However, she couldn't speak Cree so it was pretty lonely for her while I was away. The Swedish and Norwegian came from Carl, her stepfather, the German came from Louise's mother who came to the States as a child from Dusseldorf with her parents, Minnie and Albert Grefunda. Minnie was quite a character, and twice as big as her husband. When Minnie's folks died in the States, she sent Albert to settle things up. Albert didn't trust banks, so he packed the money in his suitcase. When he got to the Canadian border, he changed it to Canadian currency getting $800 more in the exchange, which he put aside for himself. When he got home Minnie offered him money for expenses but he said he would do it for nothing. When we were visiting he gave us $100 for Louis, it was then that Minnie found out about the $800, she was furious, and took hold of him by his long white hair and shook him.

"You can shake me as much as you like," he said, "But you're not going to shake that money out of me, I earned it!"

I went back to my folks and told them all that had happened to me since I had left them. Then I went to see Minnie, and she agreed to lend me a thousand dollars, telling me that if I couldn't pay her back while she was alive, I was to give it to the boys when they were old enough to make use of it. I was very grateful to her.

I had a 1914 Briscoe touring model car, which I had left at my folks when I went north. Now I used it to run around in, and look for horses to buy. I went to Bashaw the next day and told the garage man there that I wanted to sell my car, or trade it for some horses. He referred me to someone in Alix, the next town, where he thought I might be able to make a deal like that, so I went straight away. I found the man, and traded my car for two teams, getting him to throw in a bridle, I trailed them riding bareback, the twenty miles home, arriving the same night. Albert Pierson my brother-in-law, had already promised me three horses, so this made seven. The next door neighbour had bought an International Harvester tractor and was glad to sell me four head of three and four-year olds, which were only halter broken. One was a black horse, and believe me that horse gave me nothing but trouble. Altogether, I bought twenty head of horses, and I decided to trail them to save expense.

"If you're going to trail them, take my saddle pony, you'll never keep them together with any horse in your outfit, they are all strangers to each other," Albert said. I knew he was right, so I took his little horse and he sure knew his business.

The first night out I corralled the horses and fed them at a livery barn, and the next day made the sixty or so miles to Strathcona. That liveryman was a fine fellow, after I told him where I was going he insisted on riding ahead of me to show me the way through Edmonton to the St. Albert trail. I followed him down Jasper Avenue until we hit the right trail. I like to imagine the commotion it would cause if I took a bunch of horses down Jasper Avenue today!

At St. Albert, I put the horses in a farmer's pasture for the night, and put my saddle horse in a livery barn. Another forty or fifty miles brought me to Westlock, where I corralled the horses in the railroad yard for the night, and fed them some baled hay. I got into conversation with Julius Schulz, who was travelling with a carload of horses on his way to sell them to farmers at Fairview. He suggested that I load my horses too, as I couldn't travel along the lake with them. I told him that I had already wired for a car at Jarvie.

Leaving him, I trailed them to Jarvie, loaded them in a car, and we were pulled out the next day. When we got to Lesser Slave Lake, the freight waited for hours. When we got going again, we saw what had caused the delay. Three or four box cars were on their sides in the lake, and sticking up about a foot out of the water. I guess at least one contained Settler's Effects, because strutting across the side of one car was a lone rooster.

When we reached McLennan, I saw Julius Schulz who was trying to find out what the railroad intended to do about his carload of horses they had drowned. John Ward of Ft. Vermilion was also there, he was billed out to Peace River Crossing, but was held up until the next day. When he heard that I was unloading here and trailing my horses to Peace River, he decided to do the same. John was an old cowboy from the south who settled in Ft. Vermilion the year before I came to Keg River.

At Roma we found a man with a team and a wagon and ten to fifteen cows feeding in the poplar, he was just sitting on his wagon. Ward and I rode up and asked him what he was doing.

"I'm thinking" he said.

"You won't get far doing that," we told him.

"That's what I'm thinking, whether to go on or go back." He did go back, because when we received the Master Farm Family award in 1953, he wrote to me from Saskatchewan.

We arrived at Peace River and left the horses in a pasture at the top of the hill just out of town. John was taking the boat to the Fort, it had just left, and it would be a week before it was back, so I suggested that he come with me overland.

"Do you know how to find that pack-trail from Battle River to the Keg?" he asked me.

"No but I think I can get a native to come along." I said.

"Not for me," he stated, "three hundred miles on a trail, part of which you don't know, and fighting flies all the way. I'll wait for the boat!" He was quite determined. So the next morning John helped me trail my horses through the town and across the bridge, then he turned back to wait for the boat.

I arrived in Battle River that night after a trip of around ninety miles. I left the horses loose on the river bank near the village. I knew they were too tired to move far. I was wrong. That black horse was missing. It had caused me lots of trouble all along and wouldn't stay in the bunch. It kept trying to get back, and now it was missing altogether. I camped with Joe Strong a native, who said he would keep an eye on the horses while I went back to look for the black. I had already named him, and the name grew a little longer! I back-tracked and found him at Johnny Arnault's place about six miles back.

After catching the black, I went back to Joe Strong. I persuaded him to come with me and show me the trail to Keg River. His wife baked bannock, and Joe rustled up enough tea and lard, taking one of his pack ponies, we pulled out the next day.

We camped on a little prairie that night, which was a good camp for the horses, though the flies were terrible. We built a smudge and the horses stayed right alongside it, even the black, although he had tried to get back several times on the trail. After daylight it started to rain, Joe wouldn't move in the rain, and all we had to keep dry was a small tarp. I hated to stop, as I knew the horses would be restless. I told Joe this but he didn't agree, being used to packhorses who are contented to stay anywhere there is feed. Anyway I caught the black and picketed him, I had had enough of chasing him. I was soaked to the hide by the time, as I had to keep that smudge going. During the afternoon it quit raining, so we got a huge fire going to dry our clothes out.

By evening we were fairly dry, and as we sat by the fire Joe suddenly said,

"Geese!" We were camped close to the riverbank, and we crept close enough to see the water, sure enough there were four or five big geese coming down the river with twenty or thirty young geese about half-grown. In a minute we were in the river up to our necks catching young geese. I don't remember how many we caught but enough to feed us all the way to the Keg. We had just finished drying out and now we were soaked to the skin again!

We cleaned the geese, split them open, and roasted them in front of the open fire, a feast to beat all. By about three o'clock in the morning it was daylight again, I made up the smudge, the horses were still with it, and Joe had our breakfast of bannock, roast goose, and tea ready.

I made a mistake when I turned that black horse loose with the others, I should have led him. All the others followed Joe with his packhorse but not that black. He got back on me twice, and before you can get past a horse on a packtrail, you have to wait until you come to some place clear enough to put on speed and pass it. You have to go a mile or so at times.

The last time I went back for the black horse, I was jumping over windfall to get ahead of it when I fell off my horse, and knocked myself out on a tree stump. My horse waited, standing on the trail ahead of that black until I came to. I tried to catch him but couldn't so herded it back, finally catching up to Joe.

We were in small spruce and Joe kept on going until nearly sundown, when he came to some sloughs and started to make camp. I made a smudge for the horses and while we were eating supper I told Joe the trouble I had had with the black horse and that I intended to try and catch it, and picket it. Joe told me he had taken the wrong trail.

"Over there," he said, "Is the lake where Gavel lost a horse. He was trailing a bunch of horses to Hay Lakes, and got lost in these hills. The horses tried to get water, but couldn't as the edge of the lake was just a bog. One got bogged down so much he couldn't pull it out, and had to shoot it. He was out of grub so he ate horsemeat."

Horse meat makes good eating, especially if you're hungry. I went to look for the black, the horses were feeding along the slough, the black had gone, and I sure wasn't going back for it anymore, I never saw it again. Late in the fall he turned up at Johnny Arnault's place, and stayed with his horses until spring when Johnny sent me word and said if I wanted it, would I come and get it. I sent word back that he could keep it, I had seen all I wanted of that horse!

Next day we worked our way west trying to get back on the right trail. It wasn't long before I saw that Joe had found a trail going west. We followed it all day and came in sight of Keg River. We were on top of the hills and had a good view of the country. In those days when the Keg was a prairie, the country was open to the foot of the hills in the west, north to beyond Paddle Prairie, and eastwards towards the Peace, where it was scrub poplar.

These hills today are called Naylor Hills after old Dick Naylor, Revillon's trading post manager. There has been a forestry tower on these hills for many years, but in 1975 it was removed by helicopter, and the lookout closed down. Finally Joe came to the trail he should have been on, which led down off the hills, and was only about ten or twelve miles from home. We arrived there sometime during the night. Louise made us some supper, we were out of bannock but we had one goose left. I grub-staked Joe and gave him twenty-five dollars.

"That's good I feel like a millionaire!" he said.

CHAPTER SEVEN

Haying and Winter on Paddle Prairie

Next morning Pete and I collected the horses and put the likely looking ones in the corral, we were looking to see what teams we could make out of them ready to start haying. As young Louis was climbing the fence, he fell off and broke his leg below the knee. I left the horses and set it for him, making a cast out of wet newspaper strips about six inches wide, and binding on about twelve layers or so. The newspaper was The Saturday Evening Post, the only one I subscribed to, it came with the mail, and we'd get about six copies at a time. I thought the cast would do, but I kept Louis confined to the house to give his leg the best possible chance of healing, and I stayed around to keep an eye on it. It healed up completely in time, which was another hurdle overcome.

Meanwhile I left Pete to sort out the horses. In the afternoon Magloire Mercredi came up wanting flour, he had hayed for me before, so I asked him to come back and help Pete with the horses. Pete hitched two teams to a wagon and went to the river to pick up the freight I had bought in Peace River, Magloire went with him so that he could bring back the wagon that was already there. Magloire wasn't much of a teamster then, though he became one over the years. By the time they got back from the river Pete had learned a lot about the new horses.

Mercredi was a Chippewayan native, a short stout man as strong as a bull, he spoke fair English as well as French, Cree, Slavey, and Beaver. He was part of Isidore Capotblanc's clan and lived in a tepee with his wife and nine children. Isidore was a little short man, a Beaver Indian raised around here, his father died before I came to Keg River, but he kept three wives and they all lived together in one tepee. The Indians kept as many wives as they could support in the old days, they were as useful as packhorses, the women carried a huge load when they went to the bush. They carried everything in a blanket, the ends tied loose and put over their foreheads.

Eventually, when I got to know him better, I persuaded Mercredi to grow a garden, he said he knew nothing about gardens but I told him that I would plow up a small piece of land where he was camped and show him. After I got him started, he had a garden every year, and packed the vegetables into the bush when he went to his trapline with his family in the fall. I visited Mercredi a few years ago, where he was living in Hay Lakes, and he still kept a garden.

The hay was a big disappointment, it was very thin and we had to cover a large territory to get enough, at last I thought I had enough but one can never be sure. Dick Hutchings came back with a partner, Johnny Nelson, they intended to build themselves a cabin north of us, and to trap together during the winter. This meant that they didn't want the cabin we were occupying which was a help. As it got colder, it was a relief not to have any flies to cope with.

I did run short of hay but managed to get enough here and there to see me through. As spring came round I was anxious to see how the cows would make out with calving. I was lucky, although I had had only one bull, I got between thirty and forty calves. I had a lot of dry cows but I only lost one cow that was carrying a dead calf. She appeared to be suffering from the same complaint as the cows I had lost the previous year.

I went out again this spring and took Louise and the boys with me this time. Louise went to see her folks, and I stayed in Edmonton to buy next year's grubstake. It was quite a chore to figure out what we needed to see us through for a whole year.

While in Edmonton I went to the Land Office and applied for a grazing lease on township 101. They couldn't find Keg River on the map and decided that it must be in the Northwest Territories! However, they forwarded my application to Ottawa, but told me I would have to get permission from Ottawa before I could live on the land, or make improvements on it.

Going home we missed the boat in Peace River, so I bought a small boat and we went home in that. John Christian was hauling for Revillons, but one of his horses, a white cayuse had played out, so he had been at the landing for two days. He agreed to take us home and leave the freight for another trip.

John Christian was a Roumanian who came to Canada to work on the construction of the Grand Trunk Pacific Railway through the mountains. He enlisted in the army for the First World War, but arriving in Montreal with his contingent, was told that Roumania had become an enemy country, John was promptly arrested as an alien, thrown out of the army, and told to get back on the railroad or he would be interned!

They gave him a pass to Edmonton, but he was determined not to go back on the railroad, he had had enough of that, so he left Edmonton on foot. On the way to the Peace he stayed at a stopping place on the Grouard Trail which was run by Old Man Blackbird. John stayed around for a while working, and married one of Blackbird's daughters. The stopping place was losing its trade since the E.D. & B.C. had come through, so Old Blackbird decided to move. He moved overland to Battle River, and then to Keg River Crossing, where John was hauling freight for a living. He was also getting out logs for a cabin and intended to go trapping in the winter.

L'Octave Ducharme, a man whom we always called Fred, moved into the prairie with his family. He was a French-Canadian half-breed, and had a wife, one daughter, and six sons. He came from Buffalo Prairie, he was a real worker and I got on well with him. He built a cabin for himself along the river about a mile from the village, and worked for me on and off for the rest of his life.

We had to get on with the haying and both Fred and Magloire went out with the mowers to start. When they came in that night they said the hay wasn't worth cutting, it was too thin. I wondered if the cattle had been round there already and eaten up the grass so I told them to continue cutting and I would ride out to see.

That evening I met John Brown for the first time. He was a trapper and had a cabin about twenty-five miles away on a prairie the natives called Pad-

38

dle Prairie. He stopped in on his way to visit two boys who were trapping on the Peace. He told me that there was miles of hay on Paddle Prairie as high as his waist. When he left I asked him why he didn't use a horse.

"A horse is a nuisance, I'd rather walk," he said. John Brown was quite a character, and I will mention him again later.

I told Fred what John had said about hay on the Paddle, and he confirmed this as he had seen it on his way in from the Fort. The wagon trail from Ft. Vermilion to Keg River went through Paddle Prairie. Dave Anderson*had a small herd of cattle about three miles this side of Brown's cabin, and I told him what I intended to do, he said there was lots of hay, he could get all he wanted across the creek from his place.

I concluded that the growth of hay on the Keg was an annual grass and had to seed to get a crop the following year. The redtop and peavine that we had cut the first year had completely disappeared. Left to seed, it is too late to hay. We continued to hay down at the Keg, but we all agreed that it was hardly worth the trouble, as we weren't going to get enough.

Haying down at Brown's place presented lots of difficulties but I couldn't see any way out of it. My freight had come in and someone had made a hole in the five gallon can of mowing machine oil, and it was empty. This was a catastrophe. I had my suspicions as to who the culprit was, but there was nothing I could do about it.

John Christian took his tepee and his family down to the Paddle and started cutting, Blackbird went with him, and I asked him to hunt bear as I needed grease to use for mowing machine oil.

Pete and Fred and I finished stacking on the Keg, and we made less than two hundred loads of hay. Then we took another mower, a hay rake, a hay wagon, beds and grub, and we were all set to hay on the Paddle Prairie.

The bears were very plentiful, we saw them out on the prairie eating peavine every day. Old Blackbird trapped two, so we had lots of fresh meat, and his wife ran down the fat to provide grease for the mowers, bear grease is so soft we needed lots of it. When it was too wet to hay, I built a small barn. We left the hay in buckloads about a hundred feet long, and hayed until the grass was too frozen to be of any use.

John Brown returned just before we left, he tried to tell me that I would be better off doing a little trading for fur than trying to raise cows, he said he would come up to the Keg and talk about it. Then he told me about his visit to the Swedish boys. They had disappeared without trace. John had walked up to their cabin which was on the riverbank thirty miles above Ft. Vermilion. He found food frying for dinner burnt in the frypan, and the stove gone out. The table was set for two but there was no sign of the boys. Their boat was down by the river, and John searched around all day without success so he took their boat down to the Fort, reported what he had found to the R.C.M.P., and then walked home. Those boys were never found, and no-one knows what happened to them.

We fenced over the haystacks to keep the native horses off, left the machinery there, and returned to the Keg. John Christian went to the Keg

---

*Not his real name.

Crossing and built his cabin, Pete went back to the Fort, and Fred left to go trapping.

We were now living in the village, but I had planted the garden at the old place and Louise had to walk two miles to look after it. We went to take it up before it froze too hard, and we found we had been raided, when we dug up the potato hills, there was nothing. The natives had scraped around the hill, taken out the spuds, and covered up the vines again, so that they looked as if they had never been touched! It was lucky I had started Magloire gardening, for he got six sacks from his garden and let us have two of them.

We sure put in another hard winter, I collected the calves and left them with the milk cows and the bull at the Keg, for Louise to feed and water them. When Fred came in off the trapline during the winter, he helped Louise by hauling hay, this was a relief to her as it was sixty degrees below some nights.

I took the rest of the cows to winter on the Paddle, the creek went dry except for the potholes. There were plenty of them, but after the cattle had been using them for a while the water got too low for them to reach, so I had to chop a trench and pail the water up for them. I used to pound on the pail, and the cows would follow me from one pothole to another, along two miles of creek. I had to water the cows before daylight as it took me all day to haul hay, and I did this all winter.

One morning before daylight I thought I saw a bunch of horses over by the bush, but as it got lighter, I saw they were moose, there were twenty-two of them. In those days there were so many moose, you could creep up to them and shoot from forty or fifty feet away.

Although it got so cold, there wasn't much snow, and during the winter I made several trips back to the Keg for grub which Louise prepared for me. Somehow we struggled through without losing any cattle or horses.

When spring came we brought the cows back to the Keg and left them on the prairie for a week or so to watch them through calving. After most of them had calved, Pete and I collected them up, for I had decided at Pete's suggestion to take them out to the Chinchaga River**for the summer. There was good pasture there both upland and in several big sloughs, with good watering at the river.

The river was quite wide, with sand and gravel bars out in the open, with a wind that would help to keep the flies away. I ran the cattle out there for years after this, and some years I had to keep a man out there to make a smudge for the cattle. When the snow got deep in the fall, they would come home by themselves, we knew the winter had come when we saw them wandering across the prairie.

The workhorses seemed to be going downhill late in the spring, so I sold a team and Albert's pony. I heard later that they died of swamp fever except for Albert's little horse. I had a grey team Punch and Judy and a blue roan mare which survived, maybe because I kept them in the barn, and they lived for years afterwards.

**Called Hay River in those days.

CHAPTER EIGHT

First Log Home

It was quite a sight when the old men walked down the prairie, they all wore wide-brimmed French hats, bought from the Hudson's Bay store, and they wore brightly coloured sashes over their Hudson's Bay blanket cloth coats, with the fringed ends hanging down in front. Moise Richard acted as chief for the village. He was a short man with long greyish-white hair which he never combed, he also had a few whiskers here and there.

Old Moise was a grand old man who spoke good English, French, and Cree. He had been a freight hauler for Norris between Ft. Garry and Edmonton and came up here after the Riel rebellion. Moise was a good musician, and used to play his fiddle while driving the Red River carts.

Moise also played drum and danced at the tea-dances. The Indians used to crowd into one cabin for their dances, singing, dancing, and drinking penusal juice. Penusal juice was white like milk, and was made out of berries; chokecherries, pincherries, saskatoons, etc. There was no liquor here then but as long as they had berries to make penusal juice, they would be drunk. When the berries ran out, they would be sober.

I don't know how it was made, but I drank it only once. It was summer-time and I was thirsty, so Fred gave me some to drink, I could hardly see, and I don't know how I made it home, it was terrible. I never drank it again.

When the Keg River prairie was surveyed, the portion of land where most of the natives lived in the summer was set aside as Indian Village land, so I decided to ask Moise for permission to build a house there, he had built his cabin a good many years before the survey, and when I asked him he said, "Go ahead Frank, I never asked permission when I built here." I moved the buildings first, so that we had somewhere to live while we were building. Moving a log house is a simple operation, you just number the logs on each side before you take them down, and put them up again in the same order, then you have to chink again. With Fred and Magloire helping, it took us less than a month to move all the buildings onto village land.

I plowed some land along the edge of the river behind the buildings ready for the next season's garden and fenced it all in. I also built corrals for the cattle. We got out a few logs ready for the new house before we had to go hay-ing. Our building operations were always accomplished between essential chores, and it took us a couple of years or more to complete the house.

Fred helped me hew the logs, he was an expert and I learnt a lot from him. I found that hewing thirty logs down to eight inches thick was quite a job. We dug the basement with a Fresno I had brought up with me. I had to keep the basement fairly small and leave several feet of dirt to carry the sill

41

logs as I had no cement. There were no rocks on the Keg, so we had to go back on the hills west of here, to find big rocks for the foundation.

When it was finished, the house was thirty feet by twenty-five feet. It took six logs to make the walls nine feet high. We dove-tailed the corners, again Fred was the expert, and it didn't take me long to catch on, so we worked together on each log, using an axe which had to be as sharp as a razor. We made a dovetail, put up a log and rested it there, we judged the distance, and if it was five inches, then we sawed down four inches and then started the dovetail. We always allowed about an inch, which we used up getting it to fit.

I had lots of tools, most of them came from my Dad who brought them with him from England, but all we needed to build a log cabin was a hammer, an axe, and a saw.

I got Fred to fetch flooring from Sheridan Lawrence at Ft. Vermilion, Sheridan had a sawmill run by a steam engine on his ranch. Fred took the four best horses we had, he had a rough, hundred and twenty-five miles trip over a trail through the bush. The lumber we brought was one and a quarter inch thick, tongue and grooved at $35 a thousand.

The kitchen roof was made of tamarack poles which will never rot, but are hard to get straight. The main roof was made with poplar poles split with an axe. You drive an axe into the exact centre, then a second axe a little further down and so on, crawling down the pole. It is a thousand times easier to do this when they are frozen.

We bought spruce bark from the natives for the roof. The old women used to cut it, they had to walk out and find a good tree without knotholes, then they would slit the bark down at the top and bottom, and peel it off in pieces about six feet square, roll it up and carry it back on their backs. With the bark off, the spruce tree would die, and then they had firewood.

When it was green it didn't split or tear, and we laid it on the roof straight away like a carpet. When the sods were placed on top of it, the weight on the roof was tremendous, and it had to be a well built house to carry the weight. Fred helped me plow the sod for the roof, we had to haul it quite a long way, as it is hard to find clay sod on this prairie. The sods were put on grass-side down and the clay surface smoothed to encourage the water to run off. In about three years wind-dispersed seeds might lodge on it, and they would start to grow. The bark and sod roof was warm in winter, and cool in summer, the pitch of the roof was about three inches to a foot. After we had moved in, we finished the ceiling with wood from packing cases.

I made the chimney myself out of sheet iron, our stove was a huge cast iron monster which originated in Ontario. I bought it from a secondhand store in Peace River the second year I was here. It weighed seven hundred pounds, and would take a twenty-five pound roast easily, it sure held plenty of heat.

I divided the main part of the house into three bedrooms, and a sitting room. The kitchen had a pantry with a sink in it, and I made a bathroom in the basement of the kitchen, where I dug a well, and found plenty of water at fourteen feet. I made the bath out of galvanized iron, and put in a wash basin. Then I put in water tanks made out of two coal oil barrels. I had them one above the other with cold water in the top tank, and hot water in the bottom tank, and a valve between. A water-jacket in the stove gave us plenty of hot water. The overflow from the cold water tank went back into the well, the pump at the well, was an ordinary dual rotary pump turned by hand.

The water was good but built up sediment at the rate of half an inch a year in our tea kettle. In one year the water-jacket was filled up with it, and I took the edge off my hacksaw sawing it out, it was so hard. I put in one and a half inch pipes instead, and had to saw them out and replace them every year.

Apart from this the plumbing worked well for five or six years, giving us constant hot and cold water. I got the purser on the boat to pick up two lengths of six inch pipe from one of the abandoned oil wells on the way from Peace River. All kinds of pipe had been left around which deteriorated rapidly in the acid fumes from the wells. I wanted them for a drain from the house to the cesspit. We moved before I had time to put in the toilet I planned.

I made the windows with ten by twelve glass panes which came glued together with syrup, I screened the windows and doors, no-see-ums could get through the screen, so I painted them green and this made the holes just too small for them. This was better than a smudge. We still used smudges in the garden though, we'd have one at each end of the row when we were weeding, for in those days there were mosquitoes by the millions. I made a lawn in front of the house, fenced it in, and put flower beds around the fence.

CHAPTER NINE

Bears, T. A. Brick, and a Hard Trail to the Paddle

We made hay on the Paddle again, although where we had cut the previous fall much of the hay was too poor to cut, going the same way as it had at Keg River. When it was too wet to hay, I put in time damming up the creek with a slip. The creek was still running, and by freeze-up it was full to the top of the dam, giving me about eight feet of water, filling a slough hole that was on the south side of the creek as well. Old Blackbird was down again hunting bear, we would see five or six out every day feeding on the prairie.

Dave Anderson came down one day and asked me to milk his cow and build a smudge for her, while, he and his wife went down to Carcajou to fetch freight, and visit with the Rankins. I used to walk as it was only just over two miles. The second evening, I was about half-way there and passing a bluff of small poplars, when I met a full grown red bear.

I stopped short, so did the bear, and he stood there eyeing me out of one eye, with one paw raised off the ground. It was no good my thinking of running back as I was a mile from camp, and I knew he could run as fast, if not faster than I could. The poplars were too small to climb, so I just stood there, we were about fifty feet apart staring each other out. I wasn't scared, at least I thought I wasn't, but the hairs on the back of my neck were gradually standing on end. After what seemed like a long time, the bear made one step towards the bush, still with one eye on me. When he made that step, I let out a yell and charged after him, he took off like the wind and didn't look back.

Old Blackbird caught him two days later in one of his traps, we went down to help him get it across the creek. Blackbird had the trap chained to a poplar tree which was about eight inches thick, and about four feet from the ground the bear had chewed it right through! He weighed about six or seven hundred pounds, and I was thinking I'd had a lucky escape!

It was a few years afterwards that John Christian met a silver tip grizzly bear on the trail. He was walking up the Keg leading his horse when suddenly the horse snorted and pulled back. John couldn't see why, then he noticed his horse looking up, the bear was on the bank above him not fifty feet away. John raised his rifle and fired at it, when the bear started to roll down the bank, John got on his horse and beat it. After a short way, he looked back, there it was, just where he had been standing, though quite still.

John waited a while, then when it didn't move he went close, it was quite dead, so he skinned it out leaving the fat on the hide like the Indians do.

45

There was about five inches of fat, which made it too heavy to lift on his horse, so he had to ride home and fetch his wife to help him.

It was John who told me of another incident. He and Blackbird were trapping near Stoney Creek, during the spring beaver hunt. Blackbird and John were walking home together with the pack dogs. They weren't far from the river, and while the pack dogs lay down on the trail, Blackbird and John went up to the river to see if there were any beaver, Blackbird went on ahead. John couldn't see any beaver so he turned back to the trail, it was then that a commotion broke out among the dogs. A bear had hold of one of the dogs by the pack, and he was shaking hell out of it.

John put a cap on the firing pin of his muzzle-loader and fired point blank at the bear. The gun didn't fire, as he was trying to put another cap on the gun, he saw that the dog had come loose and the bear was tearing the pack which contained their beaver pelts. John shoved the gun barrel into the bear's mouth, this made the bear drop the pack, then he took a swipe at John.

Old Blackbird heard the racket and came running back. He shot the bear dead, but when he got to it, he couldn't find John. At last he found him, over the bank and completely knocked out, and as the old man said, two more rolls and he would have been in the river!

In the fall T. A. Brick and Baldy Red came into the prairie, with some horses that Mr. Brick had raised at Shaftesbury, along the west bank of the Peace River above Peace River Crossing. Mr. Brick was the son of the Rev. Gough Brick who was a missionary sent to the Peace River country from Quebec. He built a little church by the Peace at Shaftesbury, and started a farm, where all the market gardens at Peace River are now. T. A. Brick was the first Member of the Legislative Assembly for the Peace River District in 1905.

Baldy Red had a homestead just out of Peace River, and was quite a notorious character, booze-running during prohibition being his chief occupation. T. A. Brick sold some of their horses on time to the natives and turned the rest loose.

I received a letter from the Land Office to tell me that my application for a grazing lease had been turned down, as the surveyors classified it as farm land. They tried to bill me for the use of the lease, and it had taken them two years to make up their minds. My mind was made up too, after seeing the results of haying on the land, I didn't want it, though it stopped me from growing oats, which I needed to survive.

The natives hayed west of here about five or six miles, and I never encroached in that direction, though it seemed to be better hay, mostly wild rye grass, and not all fireweed as it was where I had hayed previously on the Keg.

Fred had built a little barn by his cabin so that he could keep his team in, and feed them, during the winter, as turned loose they had only just pulled through. As there was hay left on the native's hayfield he used my machinery, and with help from his boys made hay there. He was able to let me have twenty or thirty loads he didn't need next spring.

John Brown turned up again. He was on his way towards the B.C. boundary to trap. He had hoped I would be spending the winter at the Keg, as he wanted me to buy fur for cash for him. I had no choice but to spend the winter at the Paddle with my cows again, but I told him I would see what I could do. John promised me half of the profits if I would buy fur for him, and he left me three thousand dollars which was mostly in dollar bills for that purpose. He had had it cached in sealers in the ground, and it was so damp, I had to dry it out before I could count it.

Magloire Mercredi called to leave dried meat in the warehouse, I gave him a key telling him I would be away on the Paddle for the winter, and informing him of my intention to buy fur for cash this winter.

"That's good," he said, "I might come down to see you, we are going to winter on the twenty-seventh baseline again."

I took Louise, the boys, the hens, the milk cows and all the other cattle I could find down to the Paddle. About twenty cows were missing, I weaned the calves, hauled hay for Louise to feed out, and went back to look for them. My dam was holding so there was plenty of water.

It was late in the fall, Joe Kemp had given Paulis Bottle flour, and bacon, and he had agreed to go and hunt for my missing cows. He found them across the river, perhaps the natives had driven them over there to keep them out of their haystacks. Fred helped me to bring them home where we fed them, one cow was very thin and her calf was missing. I asked Fred if he would help me take them down to the Paddle, he wasn't too keen as we had had a heavy snowfall, and the weather was very cold. However, he said he didn't like to see me stuck, and agreed to come. He brought us snowshoes to wear, and I had everything packed before daylight. Fred led the way and the cows followed in single file strung out behind.

We made quite a ways before daylight, after about twelve miles we camped in some willows to eat, put down willows to sit on in order to keep our moccasins dry and stopped for about an hour. Our thin cow played out soon after we started again, so I had to leave her. The snow here was about three feet deep, and we were making a trench in the snow right across the prairie. Fred broke trail with his snow-shoes, and the horse and flat sleigh followed him, the cows followed in single file, the calves following them. I would herd them along from above on my snowshoes, and I would have to go close and look down to make sure the calves were following, for I couldn't see them otherwise. I went backwards and forwards making sure they kept on the move. It soon got dark and we still had ten miles or so to go. As it was all open prairie from now on, I didn't expect Fred to stop unless he played out. We plodded on all night breaking trail all the way.

It was getting daylight before we reached the cabin. Louise got up and put coffee on the stove, but Fred and I just flopped down on the floor and were asleep before it was ready. Louise woke us up to drink it, and I asked her to go outside and look after the horse and flat sleigh, and feed the cows we had brought, then we went back to sleep. When we came alive again, Fred and I had breakfast and supper all in one. Then I drove a team and sleigh out to haul back that thin cow. Fred rode under some blankets in the sleigh, for it was around forty below.

We arrived at the place where we'd had lunch, and failing to find the cow where she had played out, we wondered where she had got to. We stopped and fed the team and took our grub into the willows to eat, and found our cow lying frozen to death on the willows that were in front of our dead camp fire. Fred had a walk of about twelve miles to his home from here, though he had a fair trail that we had made. Plowing trail had been quite hard on the team, but it was a little easier going back.

47

The rest of the winter was the same hard routine. I hauled hay and opened the water-holes. Three cows fell through the hanging ice on a slough and drowned. That was four cows lost and the winter only just begun. Hauling hay was quite a chore as I had to shovel snow off the bunches. I asked Dave Anderson how he was making out, he said he didn't haul hay for his cows, he fed them out where the hay bunches were. That's O.K. except when the wind is blowing, then it's mighty cold out in the open for cows. I had a feedlot in the bush out of the wind.

I sure made up my mind to take some cows out after haying this summer. Magloire Mercredi and Narcise Capotblanc came down around New Year's with a dog sleigh, they said it was heavy going with so much snow everywhere. They had all made a good hunt as there was plenty of fox and mink. I told them about the cows I had lost and told them where they would get the cow that froze to death on the trail, if they wanted it for dogfeed.

They had come to sell me some fur for cash, I bought quite a few from them, taking Magloire's advice as to price and quality. They sold fur to the Hudson's Bay for trade but not for cash. They stayed the night, and left the next morning.

We had quite a few visitors after they left, native trappers coming and going between the Fort and the Keg. Pete Lizotte and his brother Billy came through, they hadn't done very well with their trapping as there weren't many fox down their way. Pete was never much of a trapper but he always had a splendid dog team which he decorated with brightly coloured woollen pompoms. I told Pete about buying some fur, he said I had to have a licence to do that.

"The posts will report you if they find out, you'd better be careful." I told him I hadn't known that. I put the fur in some sacks and got Pete to hang it in the heavy spruce behind the feed lot. Pete promised to look in again when he passed for they had traps out on the trail.

I bought quite a lot of fur that spring from the trappers when they came in. I saw old Dick Naylor and told him what I was doing, and asked him if I was interfering with his business.

"If you're interfering I'll soon tell you," he said. I also spoke to Joe Kemp the Hudson's Bay man, and he said,

"If anything is said, I'll say you're buying for me as I can't pay cash," so that was that.

CHAPTER TEN

John Brown and The Keg River Trading Company

John Brown came in, having made a good hunt, mostly fox. I showed him the fur I had bought which was hanging up in my warehouse.

"We'll sack it up and take it to the Fort," he said. I wanted him to take it to Edmonton, but he dealt with Lamson and Hubbard at Ft. Vermilion and was determined to take it there. I tried to get out of going, but he said he wasn't coming back right away, so I would have to go with him. I sure didn't want to make that trip to the Fort, but finally I had to give in and go. It wasn't much of a trail, you could get lost easily, it wandered all over. It was really a winter trail.

I gave John a horse to ride and we packed one horse. The trail was under water most of the way, but as the ground was still frozen there was very little mud. It took us three days to get there, and John took two days to sell the fur. We made four hundred dollars on it, so two hundred of it was my share. Not so much, but far better than trying to raise cows at that time when they were worth practically nothing. Harry Edgecome, the Lamson and Hubbard manager said,

"I can only pay you by draft on our Edmonton office."

"Well John," I said, "There's no way out of it, you'll have to go to Edmonton."

"No Harry, make that draft out for three thousand two hundred in Frank's name." "Frank, you put up three thousand and we'll form a company. Buy some goods and do a little trading." This was quite a thought, I didn't have three thousand dollars to begin with, but I agreed to give it a try.

We asked Harry Edgecome to draw up an agreement, we were to be called The Keg River Trading Company, capitalized at six thousand dollars, the profits to be shared equally. I just forget all the rigmarole Harry put into it, but I do remember that I knew I had let myself in for something about which I knew very little.

It took me three days to get home. I found August La Fleur at the Boyer River, he had driven his wagon into the river which was about ten feet deep, and drowned one of his horses. His wife was behind some willows drying out after being dumped in the river. I lent August the cayuse John had ridden to the Fort, to haul his wagon out of the river and get home. Arriving home, I told Louise all that had happened and what I had done.

49

That summer T. A. Brick came back to the Keg overland, to try and collect for the horses he had sold on time. I told him I was thinking of starting a trading post, and was going to Edmonton to see about supplies. T. A. Brick, or Allie as we called him, said he would help us with the building when we got back. I asked Fred to get out logs for a store and warehouse, we were in the building business again!

Whenever we went away we had to arrange for someone to look after the cattle, milk the milk cows, and take us to the boat. Pete was going to look after things at the Chin, and take us to the boat. John Christian's wife was going to milk the cows and use the milk. She knew how to milk for they had had cows at the stopping place on the Grouard Trail.

So Louise, the boys and I went to Edmonton and at Lamson and Hubbards I presented my draft. After lots of discussion and suggestions I signed a contract with the Western Grocers, who agreed to advance me three thousand dollars on credit, providing I shipped all furs to them. I was very satisfied with this deal, because it made me a full partner with John. The manager, Mr. Stewart was a fine man, and I enjoyed dealing with him.

I spent the next day at the Western Grocers giving them my order, anything they didn't stock they arranged for me to get from another wholesaler. In those days our goods came in large chests or barrels, tea came in hundred pound chests, coffee beans in hundred pound barrels, white beans in hundred pound sacks, dried fruit in twenty-five pound boxes, and jam and syrup in cans. We bought nothing else in cans, for it was too heavy to freight, and would freeze up in the store. There were no cigarettes, but we stocked Old Chum tobacco, and cigarette papers. Chewing tobacco called Niggerhead was black, and came twisted like rope in ten pound wooden caddies.

I made it clear to the wholesaler that I wanted these goods shipped north to arrive sometime around the first of September. Then I hurried back to the hotel for lunch, and we managed to catch the train which left at three, I was anxious not to miss the boat. I realized that I had forgotten to buy powder, shot and shells, but I bought them at the hardware store in Peace River, and Louise Bourassa hauled them to the boat with our groceries.

When we woke in the morning we were away downriver and the boys were racing round the deck. The boat was full of people going to the Fort, and trappers going to Little Red River just above the Chutes. We had breakfast and talked to various people. We had to stop frequently to take on cordwood which was stacked at intervals along the riverbank. Men were given contracts to cut and haul it for the Thomas's boilers, they were given two dollars a cord, the wood was spruce, cut in four foot lengths, and not more than six inches in diameter, if it was larger, it had to be split. A wooden chute was carried on the boat, and the crew shot the wood down this onto the deck, it also doubled as a gangplank. The spruce close to the bank had been cut long ago, and the men had quite a way to haul wood with horse and stoneboat. The captain measured off two or three cords, and it was loaded on the boat.

We arrived at Keg River landing after dark. The boat went across the river to tie up for the night at Carcajou Point. Pete wasn't there to meet us as expected, so I built a fire to keep us warm. We had no camp outfit, so we just had to sit by the fire. I had groceries, but no kettles. The boys slept and

Louise and I slept in fits and starts, whichever of us woke up attended to the fire.

In the morning John Christian turned up, Pete had sent him with grub and bedrolls, but they hadn't expected the boat until that day. We had a meal before we left and camped at John's place on the way back, it was a relief to get indoors out of the cold. We reached home the next night, the team were all in, even though they didn't have much of a load, I walked most of the way, and we all walked where it was good going.

Johnny Nelson thought we could get quite a lot of hay up around his cabin. Fred and Magloire brought the machinery back from the Paddle, and told me that muskrats had tunnelled through my dam and let the water out. Magloire brought his brother-in-law to help him with haying, he was a little Beaver Indian called Acquenezi, he couldn't speak a word of English, so Magloire was his boss, and he didn't think much of him. Magloire did the work of two men stacking, he was sure a good worker. With Fred on the mower and myself running the bucking pole, we managed to get quite a lot of hay.

We put up a haystack close to Dick Hutchings cabin. There were thousands of rabbits that fall and they took up residence in and around the haystack, and they ate and tunnelled into the stack so much that eventually the wind toppled it over. Dick said it was sure handy for him, he would go out with his muzzle loader, shoot alongside the stack, and get twelve or fourteen rabbits with one shot.

CHAPTER ELEVEN

Fishing

During the summer Allie, Louis, and Art put in most of their time fishing in the Keg. All Art had to fish with was a safety pin with a grasshopper for bait, but they all caught fish, mostly grayling trout about half a pound in weight.

A visiting native told us that there were lots of fish in the Wolverine River, a tributary of the Peace not far from Carcajou Point. The fish were goldeyes, which resemble small whitefish, and weigh up to two pounds. As soon as Allie heard this he was all set to go back with him to fish, hoping to borrow a net from the natives. Allie was really at home with the natives being able to speak Cree as fluently as they could. He caught three barrels of fish, salting them and filling the barrels with water.

I had to go to the river around the first of September to meet the boat, and Allie gave me two barrels of fish to take home, he had a third one he wanted to keep and take home to Peace River for himself, when he went back on the boat. Until then we buried it in the mud near the warehouse.

When I got my fish home, I made a proper brine for them, I used the same brine I used for bacon. I put salt in boiling water, let it cool down and poured it over the fish, after it had settled and floated all the foreign elements off the fish, I skimmed it, drained it off and boiled it again. The brine was strong enough when it could float an egg. Sometimes I would have to boil it a couple of times before it was crystal clear. Some of these fish were good to eat two years later.

Just before freezeup I took Allie to the river to catch the last boat. We saw him off with his barrel of fish, which to my mind smelt a little high. Allie claimed they were just right for him! Allie was always delighted when we were travelling if he found chuckeggs to cook, if they were half-hatched, sprinkled with a little salt, there was nothing like them according to Allie!

The following year when Allie came with his daughter Emma, our boys were waiting for him, they had seen fish in the Keg, the water was very low, only about two or three feet deep, and it was alive with suckers. These fish cannot be caught with a hook for they are bottom feeders. By this time I had bought a net, so I turned the fishing chore over to Allie who made a trap. They had great fun and caught about a hundred, split down the back, packed in brine for twenty-four hours, rinsed off and smoked, they were as good as smoked cod, and kept for a year or so.

One day the kids were down at the river, taking fish out of the trap, I heard a yell, and ran down to see what had gone wrong. It appeared that the kids had handed Emma a fish, it had flopped out of her hands, and she had

53

jumped into the river after it. The yell I heard was when she hit the water, the boys were up to their necks in the river, and having a great laugh at Emma's expense.

Allie's fish gave me an idea, I would put a cellar under the new warehouse and fill it with ice to keep the stuff cool. I did this that winter, and we had ice through the summer. When it melted it was standing in water, and this made it melt more quickly. I didn't put ice in the cellar again, I put it up on the floor which was made of poles, and covered it with hay, this kept it in good shape, for ice has to have air around it to keep.

One fall I visited the trappers at Bowe's house on the Chin and found that Johnny Nelson had been fishing in a slough, and had caught forty or so jackfish about four feet long. The fish had got into the sloughs at highwater and were stranded when the river went down. I had seen this happen in a slough down below Rainbow Lake portage, a native called Antoine Bottle was trapping there when he saw steam coming up out of a hole in the ice, so he went over to investigate. There were so many fish, they were keeping the hole open, so he sat down and figured out a way to catch some.

Antoine took the handle off his tea kettle which was a five pound lard pail, straightened it out and tied it to a pole. He took a piece of red duffel off his moccasins, tied it around the end of the wire and then put it in the hole. He found that all he had to do was plunge it in, and pull it out right away, this way he caught a good supply of fish for himself and his dogs. He made several trips that winter for fish, though the next winter there were none, I expect they managed to get over the sand bars and into the river.

The same fall, when it got cold, and there was a little snow, I went with Allie to Sheridan Lawrence's for a load of flour. On the way back we camped on a bank of the Paddle River across from Eleske, an Indian village west of where Rocky Lane is now. It was brilliant moonlight, and after supper we sat by the fire. Suddenly Allie said,

"Listen!"

"What is it?" I asked.

"It's fish," said Allie, "They're going down the river." We stood on top of the riverbank and looked. The river was in pools, nearly dry and not frozen over. Sure enough, grayling trout, with the moon shining on them, were jumping from one pool to another. They would flip along, lay still a minute and then go on again, always in the right direction.

"Bring the waterpail," said Allie, "We'll go down and catch some for breakfast." In a short time we had caught a couple of dozen.

The moon had set, and it was dark when we woke in the morning, and one of the horses had got loose. I had to hunt all over for it, but I found it at last with a bunch of Indian cayuses. When I got back Allie had the other horses harnessed, and our breakfast of fresh trout, bannock and tea ready to eat.

CHAPTER TWELVE

Trailing Cattle to Grimshaw
with Dick McGrane

Dick McGrane who was living on a flat of the Peace River below Car- cajou Point, had a small bunch of cattle, also some sheep, and he did a little trapping for a living; he came up to see me.

"Frank, I hear you are going out overland with some cows, I have about forty head of cows I want to sell, I wondered if I could come along with you?"

"Dick, what about your sheep?"

"I had forty-six sheep, but I sent forty of them up on the D. A. Thomas, and all I got out of them after paying all expenses, was a suit of underwear and a can of tobacco, and I put up hay for them for years."

"Did you save the six to start raising more?"

"Not likely, I'm going to kill them this fall."

"O.K. bring your cows up as soon as you can, and we'll go out together."

Sam Baptiste Wanuch and his wife agreed to go with us, they would go ahead of the cows with two packhorses. Everything was arranged, and when Dick arrived with his forty cows, we set off. We had two hundred head of cat- tle altogether including calves. We had a difficult time getting them across the river, as there was no trail only a steep bank. Once across we didn't loiter, but pushed them along to a prairie about ten miles from home, at the foot of the hills. It was easier to hold them, and stop them from going back on a prairie. Here we camped for the night and had to build several smudges right away, as the flies were out in droves.

Sam and his wife camped at one side of the fire, and Dick and I at the other, we each cooked for ourselves. I did the cooking for Dick and me. The first night out, I tried to cook some white beans, they came out of the pot as hard as they went in, so I kept them, and tried to cook them again the next night. We kept trying to cook these beans all the way to Grimshaw, but they were still as hard as ammunition when we threw them away.

Sam had a little dog along with him, he was called Bobby, and he was sure smart. Sam used him on the spring hunt, and if a rat sank in the water Bobby would dive down and bring it up. He never barked at the cattle, packdogs and sleigh dogs are trained not to bark. When we made camp, Sam gave the dog his tea kettle, and told him to go and get water, if it was a bit weedy he'd send him back and tell him to get some clean water, and Bobby would go back and bring clean water. The dog never came to our side of the fire, he was a real one man dog. Sam left a spoon in one camp twelve miles back, he showed Bobby a spoon and told him to go back and get it, in the morning he was back with the spoon.

The next day we went only as far as a creek on top of the hills. Sam knew the country and the best places to camp. The water was still running in the creek but it was hard for the cattle to get water as the mud banks were about three feet high, but in time they got enough, and there was plenty of grass for feed. After supper Sam asked,

"Have you got a gunny sack?" We had one with spuds in it.

"Tip them out," said Sam, "I think we might catch some fish, the water is still running, and maybe they haven't all gone downstream." He went to look at his sack before breakfast next morning and came back with half a sackful of grayling trout. After enjoying fried trout for breakfast, we gathered the cows up and followed Sam.

Dick took half a dozen or so and went after Sam, the rest followed single-file down the pack-trail. I took a tally as they went past. This time I figured we were one short, but as we had the cows moving we kept going. The next camp was on Stoney Creek where the cows could walk right into the water and drink. We hadn't come far, only five or six miles, but Sam said the next camp was too far.

I told Dick we were one short and we'd better try and get another count now while the cows were feeding. Dick came back to say that it was one of his cows that was missing, a runt of a two-year old heifer that gave him lots of trouble coming up to the Keg.

We all went to look for her and found her in a creek. We got her out, and Dick said,

"I'm going to chase her and show her how to move!" Away ran Dick like a mad thing, and Sam and I followed walking behind. When we got back to camp, Dick said,

"Where have you fellows been? I have made up the smudges and been sitting here for half an hour."

"Is that so Dick? and where's the heifer? Did you bring it back, or did you lose it again?"

"It's out there, and I've decided to sell it," he said.

"We know that Dick, that's why you brought it along."

"No, I mean I'm going to sell it right now."

"Oh, and who is going to buy it?"

"You are Frank, you can get it so cheap, I'm tired of owning it."

"Very well, how much?"

"Ten dollars."

"Ten dollars! I'll give you eight."

"It has already cost me two dollars going back for it, are you trying to steal it? Ten dollars." No sale.

We made a long drive the next day, it was almost dark when I came into camp, Sam and Dick had made smudges for the cattle and horses. The animals didn't get much feed that night, most of the feed was in a swamp and the flies were worse than thick.

At suppertime Dick brought up the subject of the heifer again.

"Well, are you going to give me ten dollars for my heifer?"

"I wouldn't give you one dollar for it tonight, and we don't even know if we have it in the bunch!"

"Well Frank, sleep on it, and tell me in the morning."

We pulled out at daylight, and had a long drive ahead to a prairie on the head waters of the First Battle. *On this drive we were plagued by bulldog flies; they just about drove the cattle crazy. Every so often, the cattle, their sides streaming wlth blood, would charge into the willows to brush them off. Our horses didn't suffer so badly, as we kept them well-greased with a mixture of pine tar, and bear-grease, the flies couldn't get a grip on this, so the horses got some relief. By the time I arrived, Dick and Sam had made camp and got the smudges going, Dick was cooking the last of the trout for supper.

"Well Frank, are you going to buy that heifer? Trailing along behind by yourself, you've had plenty of time to think what a bargain you're getting."

"Yes, I've given it lots of thought, and I concluded it wasn't even worth eight dollars. You think there is nothing to do back there, well you've to keep heading off into the bush after a cow and a calf here, and one there, all wanting their dinner, and as for your heifer, don't mention it to me, she was lost twice, and my price is now six dollars."

"Come and eat your supper and you'll feel better," said Dick tactfully.

This was a good camp on a big prairie, so we decided to stay over the next day to give the cows a chance to fill up, as we wanted to keep them in as good a shape as possible. Cattle fatten on this peavine faster than on anything you can feed them, but they also lose it faster than you can put it on when they are being trailed or shipped. Sam went out hunting, Dick put in his spare time trying to convince me that if I wanted to make money I should buy his heifer from him.

Pulling out of this camp we had to cross the river, it was shallow with a rocky bottom and about two hundred feet wide. I asked Dick to stay back and count the cattle as they crossed the river, while I horsed them along. He did this and found one short. As his heifer was there, he thought he must have made a mistake. If it was one of mine, I figured that she would soon catch up, not liking to be alone. We finally came out on Battle River Prairie. We travelled a few miles down this, and then camped by a creek, where the cows could get water.

The camp was close to a homestead where Ring Reid lived. He was a war veteran, and had just taken up the homestead. Dick and I rode over to see him. While we were there, Ring decided it was cold and proceeded to light a fire in a heater, that seemed to be full of junk. A neighbour, Bob Henderson, another war veteran, came in and when he heard the fire going, he jumped up, put a glove on, reached into the stove and hauled out a bottle of moonshine!

The boys had just returned from running out this moonshine when we arrived, not knowing who we were, Bob had cached this bottle in the stove. The bottle rescued, we had a drink all round. Dick and I stayed until that crock died. As we left, we told the boys that we were staying over another day to give the cows a rest, and would visit them again the next day before pulling out.

---

*The First Battle River is now called Notikewin, the Second, Hotchkiss, and the Third, Meikle, or maybe it's the other way around depending on where you live and which way you're travelling!

The next morning we could see a team of cayuses outside Reid's place, so didn't go over until they left. When we arrived Reid said,

"I bought you some moose meat from a native, I thought you could do with it."

"We sure can, what do we owe you for it?"

"Well I gave him a sack of Old Chum tobacco, and it costs 35¢, so you owe me that."

"That's perfectly ridiculous!" I said.

"Not at all," said Reid, "He was perfectly satisfied."

We packed the moose meat back to camp to Mrs. Sam, who said she would dry it out, she went to work right away. It was a whole hind quarter and weighed a good hundred pounds. We decided to camp over another day to get the meat dry, and after we had got some flour from Ring Reid, Mrs. Sam baked us some bannock, for we were getting low. Ring told us that there was a store down on the Third Battle where the old trading post was, and showed us where Bob Henderson lived.

The cows were alright, and no trouble, for you could see them for a mile away. We made a smudge for them in the evening, for by then the flies got pretty bad. We rounded them up and brought them into the smudges, then we called it a day. As we sat by the fire, Sam came back, the first thing he said was,

"Looks like you fellows made a good hunt, lots of meat."

"If we left it to you, we would starve to death!' we told him, I rolled in for the night, but Dick never gave up.

"Well Frank, what about that heifer, you going to buy it?"

"No, and I didn't even see it today." He left that subject and tried another.

"You know, that crock came from Bob Henderson's place, I think we'll go over there first thing in the morning."

"O.K. by me," I said, and went to sleep.

After breakfast next morning, we decided to walk over to Bob Henderson's place, we talked for a while and finally Bob said, "Would you boys like a drink of that squirrel juice?" "We thought you'd never ask," we said. "O.K. I'll go and hunt some up." He must have been a good hunter because he soon came back with a crock. We stayed around there until late in the afternoon drinking squirrel juice, and listening while Bob told us of his exploits during the war. He was a Scotsman, a bachelor, and had been a sergeant in the army. He was a great friend of mine for the rest of his life. We left Bob and went back to get ready to move on in the morning.

We went to Johnny Arnault's place to camp that night, a good place to hold the cows, and not too far — about twelve or fifteen miles. I knew the country pretty well around there by now, and I knew we had to ford the Third Battle so I suggested to Dick that we should try and get a good count on the cows, as they crossed the river. We both came out one short according to my written tally. It was a dry cow of mine, and I couldn't fathom why it didn't come along and catch up. It must have got left behind, in the small spruce where the bulldogs were so bad.

The following year Ring Reid sent up word that he'd seen my cow, he was out trapping along that trail, and towards spring went up to some sloughs to look for signs of beaver, and found the red cow with a calf. She had

58

wintered in the sloughs, bedding down in the spruce at night, it was lucky the wolves hadn't found them. So, that cleared up the mystery of the missing cow, she had snuck off to calve.

We camped at Arnault's place where there was a good prairie, then we had a long drive to Bosman's Lake which was all swamp. It was easier for the cows now, as we had a wagon trail to follow. The flies were very bad and we needed big smudges in camp. The next drive brought us to Whitemud river, where there was a fair place to hold the cows, and for them to feed. Sam said that we could manage from there on, as it was a good road and open country. It was only twenty-five miles to Bear Lake (Lac Cardinal) where there was lots of pasture for the cows, so he turned back in the morning.

Dick took our packhorses and went out on the lead, they were used to hitting the trail by now and gave very little trouble. It was sundown before we reached the lake.

The following day I left Dick to look after the cows, and I rode into Grimshaw to see about the cars. Grimshaw was named after Doctor Grimshaw who was practising medicine in Peace River. Grimshaw had several newly opened stores, otherwise it was a mudhole studded with balm trees. The railroad had reached Grimshaw and beyond by now. We had to wait four days for cars, so I bought grub, and we camped by the lake, there were millions of ducks but we had no gun with us.

Four days later we loaded the cattle, and the train pulled out. I anticipated trouble at the divisionals by leaping out and fighting it out in the agent's office right away, they remembered me, however, they billed us through. In the caboose Dick asked the train crew if he could use their stove after they had finished their breakfast.

"Yes," they said, "But not our dishes."

"That's nice of you to let us use your stove, but I don't want to use your dishes, they don't look clean enough." Dick replied. I held my breath, fully expecting they would then refuse to let us use their stove but nothing was said.

Our next and final stop was Edmonton, what a relief! As the cattle were unloaded and looked after by the yards, Dick and I went to find some transport to town, we found someone to take us to the King Edward Hotel. There we cleaned up, and stored our camping outfit in the basement and went to bed. We hadn't slept much for two nights. We arranged to meet next morning about eight, to go down to the yards.

CHAPTER THIRTEEN

Smallpox

All the fellows from the north seemed to stop at the King Edward, and over the years I met some interesting people there. One night it was so full, the only place I could find to sleep was next to the furnace, where I rolled up in my eiderdown.

Dick and I hired a taxi to take us to the yards, where we went to the office, to find out which pens the cattle were in, and whether they had shipped any dead ones. We cut out Dick's cattle, put them in a separate pen, and counted them all. We were only one short and that was the cow I had missed on the trail, even Dick's heifer was there.

"You've still got that heifer Dick," I said to him.

"Yes, you sure lost a chance to make some money on her," he replied. We went back to the office, there the manager told us to go back to town, and forget about the cattle for today, as it was better for them to rest and get filled up, before he would put them up for sale. So to town we went. When I got back to the King Edward that evening I found Dick.

"Frank, there's some farmers staying here, and they invited us up to their rooms to play poker." I knew nothing about poker, or any other card game, they have never interested me.

"I'm not going, are you?"

"Yes, I can sure show those farmers something about it. Lend me twenty-five dollars, and I will give it back to you in the morning." I gave it to him.

At breakfast he was very quiet, and didn't say anything until we had finished eating, then he said,

"Frank, can you pay for this, I'm cleaned out." I paid, and we went to the yards. The calves had been sold. The cattle looked a bit better, as they had filled up a little. On the way to watch the brand-reader at work I noticed two cows with one of my brands on them, I realized that they were two of a bunch of five heifers I lost the year I moved north. When the brand-reader wasn't too busy I asked him about them. He said,

"If I were you, I wouldn't claim them, the freight and yard charges will come to more than the cows will sell for!" I thanked him for his advice, and decided to forget all about them. We killed time around the hotel and towards evening Dick persuaded me to lend him another twenty-five bucks to play poker again. He was quite sure that tonight, he would really show those guys a trick or two.

Poor Dick! That evening I talked to the night clerk, who confirmed my suspicion that those 'farmers' were 'card sharps', they had been staying in the hotel for a month or more. In the morning I paid for breakfast again. When we got to the yards we found that my cows had been sold.

We met a man who was looking over the young stock, with a view to buying them, he said to me,

"There's something wrong with that country you've moved into."

"Why do you say that?" I asked him.

"Well, look at these yearlings, they are too fine in the bone."

"I used the best bulls I could get," I told him.

"Well some are a fair size, but there are lots of runts." He wasn't telling me anything I didn't know, and I knew lots that he didn't, for instance, all the large ones were two-year olds, though being de-horned it was difficult to tell their age. Dick's cattle weren't sold yet, but we went and asked for an advance on our cattle. Dick paid me back the money he owed me, and told me he was finished with those 'farmers'! I went to visit Louise's grandmother and paid her back the money she had loaned me, it was the last time I saw the grandparents, for they had passed away before I went again.

Back in Edmonton the following day, I heard that my cattle had all been sold, but not Dick's. I settled up at the yards the next day, my cattle averaged fourteen dollars and eighty cents a head, after all expenses. The manager told Dick there was a buyer out looking at his cattle, I left them to it, and went to visit Dr. Brander at Strathcona.

Back at the hotel Dick told me, he hadn't sold his cattle he had given them away. He showed me the yard bill with everything itemized, and I averaged it out. It came to twelve dollars and twenty cents clear, not counting our trip to Grimshaw.

"Just a minute Dick, what's this item here? 'One two year old heifer, eight dollars,' and the freight works out to seven dollars a head. That means you got one dollar for that heifer, after all our troubles, you should've taken the eight dollars when I offered it to you! Never mind Dick, it's train day tomorrow, let's clear out of here." We sure did, we collected our camping gear and headed for the train as fast as we could, we'd had enough of civilization.

When you figure it out, the fellow who got 35¢-worth of Old Chum tobacco for his quarter of moosemeat, was getting a good price for it! Cattle prices were sure bad.

On the train I thought of what Dr. Brander had told me. Dr. Brander was an old friend of mine. As well as being a good doctor, he was a marvellous horticulturist, and he created the peony rage in Edmonton. In his garden which was called The Silver Heights Peony Farm, he had over two thousand blooms at one time. Unfortunately the garden is no more, but I still have peonies blooming at Keg River that Dr. Brander originally gave me. We had a look around his garden, his pet project at the time was iris, and they looked as if they had acclimatized well. We always had a good talk when we met, but this time he had some bad news, there was smallpox at Ft. Chipewayan. As the boys hadn't been vaccinated he gave me some vaccine to vaccinate them as soon as I got home.

I found things in a tumult on the prairie. Smallpox had been rampant for a week or so. Both boys were sick, though the disease hadn't advanced enough for me to be sure they had smallpox. I told Louise about the vaccine

Dr. Brander had given me, but we thought it was unwise to vaccinate them considering the state they were in, we would wait and see how they were in the morning.

We stayed up all night with the boys, the water from our well was really cold, so we kept their fever down with cold water. The next morning we could see the pox was beginning to appear on both of them, so now we knew what we were up against. We bathed them with iodine to reduce the itching, and continued the cold water treatment. We had an anxious time, but they pulled through with only a few scars.

The natives surely did suffer, Fred kept his family at home, and they missed the smallpox, but one Beaver family, father, mother, and five children all died. Louise and I went all over the prairie, but didn't catch it. The natives were too sick to feed their dogs, so I collected up about twelve of them, tied them up, and fed them milk for I had plenty. Altogether about forty of the natives died of smallpox. While I had been away, Fred had hauled the lumber for my flooring from the Fort, and I had a hard time to keep it, for they all wanted it to make coffins. I gave them my barn doors instead.

A man called Shorty Griffiths came through the Keg during the epidemic, he was on his way to sell horses in Hay Lakes. A party of Slaveys found him in camp not far from Hay Lakes too ill to move. They left a woman to look after him, and took the horses to Hay Lakes to feed them. Soon after Shorty arrived in Hay Lakes smallpox broke out, and many people died there also.

August La Fleur caught smallpox, and they thought he was going to die, the priest gave him the last rites through the window. However, he recovered, it sure made a mess of his face, though it didn't spoil his sense of humour. Father Quemeneur, a priest from the Fort, and quite a guy in his way, came in once by dogteam, he was no match for August. August used to make homebrew and everybody knew it. One day while every native was at church, August knocked on the door, opened it a little, and pushed his arm round the door holding up a gallon jug. In minutes, the whole shebang piled out of the door, leaving the priest standing in an empty room! Another time August swiped Joe Kemp's homebrew and refilled the barrel with slough water, he thought that was a huge joke.

CHAPTER FOURTEEN

School Books for the Kids, and a Life Saved

A family from Saskatchewan named Rankin, had rafted down the Peace intending to go to Ft. Vermilion. They were quite a large family, five boys and three girls if I remember rightly, and they had one cow, one team and some pigs. They got frozen in at Carcajou, so they eventually settled across the river from Carcajou Point on a flat above the landing where our warehouses were, there they built a log house on the edge of a big spruce grove.

While waiting for the boat one day, I walked up the river and came to their place. Outside the house resting against a wall, I saw an improvised chalkboard with school work on it. I said to Mrs. Rankin,

"It looks as if you're operating a school."

"Well," she said, "I have to try and teach the younger ones something, though it's quite a chore without any books." I admired her efforts, and I told her that the next time I was in Edmonton, I would try and get her some books from the Education Department.

The Head of the Department I found was a Mr. Nichols, I had known him in Medicine Hat where he was secretary of the hardware store where I had worked. We discussed the matter, and he said I could have anything I needed. Eventually it was decided that I would take Grade Five books, one copy of each subject, and the children could share them. I came away with an armful, all donated. Mr. Nichols told me to come back and see him the next time I was in Edmonton, and tell him how they got on. Mrs. Rankin was extremely grateful when I gave her the books, especially as books were promised for the following year also.

During the winter when I had been at the Paddle, Dave Anderson had asked me to go and look at his boy, he was about twelve years old, and Dave said he had fallen off the hayrack and hurt his back. When I looked at him I thought he had T.B. of the spine, I told Dave there was nothing I could do, he ought to be taken to Edmonton.

Dave had asked me for help once before, I think it was the second year I was here, he came over one evening late in the fall, I hardly knew the man then. He said his wife was trying to have a baby, and had been for the last three or four days, and would I go and help her.

"You're a cattle man, you can help her yourself." I told him, but he said he just couldn't tackle her. We travelled the twenty-four miles through the

65

night, and it was morning when we got there. It was the first time I had met Mrs. Anderson, who was a big woman weighing about two hundred pounds.

"I'm going to lie here and die unless you can get this baby away," she said. I couldn't leave her there to die, and Dave was too scared to touch her.

As far as I could tell the head hadn't come down properly, it was caught against the pelvic bone. If someone had been there to straighten it when she first went into labour, she would have been alright. The only tool I had with me was a hook I made myself out of a hayrake tine. It was razor sharp, and if one of my cows was in difficulty with a dead calf, I could cut a head, or a limb off a calf as easily as anything with it. Dave came in with a block and tackle.

"If you can't get it any other way Frank, we'll put this on the end of the bed."

"We don't need any block and tackle, take it away," I told him, "We'll do just the same as we do with the cows." I tied a rope to the rafters, and hoisted her feet up to the ceiling so that the baby would go back in, I could then straighten up the head, and let her down again, it was easy then to get the baby out. It was black, and blue and green, and I gave it to Dave telling him to take it out and bury it or something.

All I had for disinfectant was Creolin, fortunately Mrs. Anderson had a douche, so I was able to get a pretty good pressure to wash her out. I got the afterbirth and washed her out two or three times. I left for home the next evening, it was months before I saw her again, I was sure thankful she recovered.

When I went to Edmonton in the summer, I told Dr. Brander about the Anderson boy, and he introduced me to Dr. Edgar Allen, Dr. Allen said he would treat him free, but Dave would have to pay hospital expenses, and be prepared for him to be there for a long time.

The boy was admitted to hospital, and when Dr. Allen saw me again, he told me that he had a lot of old toys and games put away, that his children had finished playing with, and he was going to take them to the hospital for the boy. I told him it would be more beneficial If he took him a slate and pencil, and he learned to read and write, for he could do neither. He agreed with me but said,

"Who is going to teach him?" I told him of my exploits down at the Department of Education, he suggested that I go back there and see the Deputy Minister of Education, this was Dr. McNally. I had met Dr. McNally when he was a highschool teacher in Medicine Hat. He remembered me, and I told him about the Anderson boy, and my talk with the doctor. Dr. McNally said he would like to help if possible, and he consulted with the Minister, a Mr. Brown, member for Cypress Hills, whose office was just next door. They told me that they had no jurisdiction over the Edmonton Department of Education, and the teacher would have to come from them, however, they promised to get in touch with them and see what could be done. They kept their promise, and it was arranged for a teacher to go to the hospital every Wednesday afternoon, to teach the Anderson boy to read and write.

The following year Dave Anderson took his boy out of hospital, and left the country without paying his bills. When I saw Dr. McNally I told him how Dave had behaved.

"Never mind Frank, we gave the boy a good start, at least he can read and write." I then explained to Dr. McNally how the books I had taken to

Mrs. Rankin were beyond her, and if I now took Grade Six books, she would be in a worse predicament than ever. How would it be, I suggested, if I took examination papers back with me, so that the kids could fill them out at the end of the year and send them back to Edmonton, someone could check them and send them back.

McNally agreed that it was a good idea, and promised that if we sent them in, he would see if something could be worked out. Mrs. Rankin did send them in, and Dr. McNally had them checked and returned with advice on how to continue with the studies, so Education by Correspondence was born.

One winter I took our boys down to Ft. Vermilion to go to school. Sheridan Lawrence had enough children to have a school of his own with his eldest daughter teaching them. When they took correspondence lessons later, we made it a rule that they had to start school work at nine o'clock every morning.

CHAPTER FIFTEEN

A Perilous Sled Trip

It was early in the year of 1925 that Pete came in to tell us that Ambrose Hamelin just coming off his trapline, had brought news that the families camping at Slavey Lake were all sick with 'flu'. They had been unable to visit their traplines for eight or ten days, and were out of grub except for a little meat.

"Why didn't you tell Ambrose that he could get some grub to take out to them tomorrow?" I asked.

"Ambrose is going on home to Carcajou Point and he doesn't know when he will be going back to Slavey Lake. I think maybe we'd better take grub out to them tomorrow. There's four families, about twenty-five people altogether." I had no wish to take off with dog teams in this cold weather, and deep snow, over a trail I didn't know.

"That's a tall order," I said, "Which trail did Ambrose come in on? I don't know that country."

"I didn't ask him," said Pete, "I know he traps out west towards the B.C. boundary, but that's nearly a hundred miles from here. Maybe the best way would be to go down the Chinchaga River to where Isidore Capotblanc and Magloire Mercredi are trapping on the baseline, and turn west there."

We loaded up the toboggans with four, twenty-five pound sacks of flour, lard, syrup, sugar, baking powder, a little tobacco, some ammunition, matches, and candles. We left Louise to feed the cattle, and set off first thing in the morning. We had about one hundred and fifty pounds of supplies on each toboggan, plus our bedrolls, our own grub, and dog feed for four days.

Pete and I had good teams with four dogs a piece, Blackie, my wheel dog was especially good, and must have weighed nearly a hundred pounds. The wheel dog travels in front of the other three, and follows the dog driver's directions. We yelled Gee to turn them to the right, and Haw to turn them left.

It was intensely cold, but the trail was good, with no fresh snow. We reached the Chinchaga by daybreak, and headed down onto the river. The well-travelled trail saved miles by cutting across some of the big points in the winding river. We reached the baseline by dark, and stayed overnight in Isidore's cabin.

Narcise Capotblanc came over from his cabin wanting to trade his foxes for some supplies. Pete explained to him that we couldn't trade as we were taking the grub out to families who were sick at Slavey Lake. Pete asked him about the trail to Slavey Lake, and he said it was good all the way, they'd been trapping out towards there. We slept on the floor until morning.

Old Mrs. Isidore made tea for us, and gave us boiled moosemeat to eat with our bannock and lard, and then we were on our way again.

"Next time we come this way," grumbled Pete, "I'm going to bring some number one traps to catch those bugs that came out of the cracks in the floor, they bothered me all night!"

"They never bothered me, I guess they couldn't find a way into my bedroll." I told him.

By daylight we'd done five or six miles, and then the trail ended. In the direction of Watt Mountain we could see a trail that must have been Narcise's trapline, but down on the river, there was nothing.

"Well what do we do now?" I asked, "Abrose evidently didn't come in this way, there must be two feet of snow over the old trail. That's too much for the dogs with these heavy loads, let's go back and trade this grub to Narcise and Isidore, and go back home."

"I sure hate to do that when Georgie Bottle's outfit are all sick and starving. We could make it if we broke trail for the dogs. I'll go ahead," volunteered Pete. Pete plowed steadily ahead on his snowshoes, the trail was better but the dogs were still breaking through down to the hard trail underneath. After about ten miles, we changed over but my snowshoes were narrower than Pete's, and the snow kept catching on the sides of the toboggans.

The dogs were getting tired, but we didn't stop for a lunch, we kept on until we came to an old cabin with no door, where the trail to Slavey Lake turned south, it was almost dark already and bitterly cold. Pete had difficulty finding the trail, he walked back and forth trying to feel where the hard-packed snow of the old trail lay under two feet of fresh snow.

"Let's camp in this cabin for the night," I said, "We've done enough for one day, and it must be thirty below at least." But Pete had just found the trail he was searching for.

"It's only about fifteen miles now to the other lake, we can make it in the moonlight, we'll be there by night."

We started off again with Pete breaking trail, but the dogs were getting too tired, and finally we had to stop, they were all in. We neither of us knew the trail or the good camping places, so we stopped in the middle of a muskeg. The only firewood was the little dead spruce six feet high at most, and two or three inches through. We had to make do with them, they hardly made enough fire to cook by, but we cooked the dog's supper and fed them a porridge of cornmeal with a few meat scraps thrown in. We scooped a depression in the snow in front of each dog and poured in the boiling feed, about six pounds per dog. The dogs were smart, they licked it round the edges where the snow cooled it, that way it didn't freeze solid before they finished it either.

We ate fried bacon and thawed bannock, and drank tea, then we put small spruce by the little fire, and rolled up in our bedrolls on top of them. There weren't enough branches to bed the dogs down, they had to curl up in the bare snow. In the morning it was as if we were at the bottom of a well, the fire had melted through the snow and right down to the moss, and it was cold. We pulled out the little spruce from under our bedrolls, made up the fire, thawed some bannock, and made a pail of tea.

We left at daylight, and a few hundred yards down the trail we came to a fire-killed spruce bluff, with plenty of good firewood, it would have been a perfect place to camp if only we'd known. We made the trapper's cabins by noon, nobody was around, but we could see by the tracks that somebody had just left. We went into the first cabin and found an old woman, who was sure glad to see us. She made us some tea with a few leaves in some hot water, Pete went out and brought in a handful from our supplies. The other women and children came in to see us, they said the men had just pulled out without grub, hoping to find a moose.

They all seemed to be getting better, though some of the children were still out of commission. We stayed the night and the next morning I told Pete to stay until the hunters returned but I must get back, I didn't expect any trouble now the trail was broken out.

It was sixty miles to the camp at the baseline and I was planning to go straight through without stopping. It was getting really cold so I ran behind my dogs, they were making good speed, the trail made by the heavy toboggans had frozen hard and they were running on top, not breaking through.

I got as far as the fire killed spruce bluff, still racing along, when my snow-shoe caught on a snag, or broken-off branch, and threw me forward onto another snag. This drove right through my heavy clothing for about three inches into my knee joint. The snag was about as thick as my thumb and the pain was shocking. I straightened up and yelled at the dogs to stop, hanging onto the line on the toboggan.

It was no time and no place to hang around, I struggled onto the toboggan, sat on the grub box, and pounded my feet as well as I could for the pain, to keep them from freezing. The dogs drove the three or four miles to the cabin we had passed on the way in, I went inside and made a fire in the little mud fireplace. When I had thawed out a bit, I took off my clothes to see what I had done to my knee. My underwear was soaked with blood and it was still bleeding heavily. There was a big hole alongside my kneecap, full of burnt wood. I scraped out the biggest pieces of wood with my jack knife, melted a little snow to wash it off, and filled the hole with a piece of Royal Crown soap I had found on the window sill. I hoped it would stop the bleeding, and perhaps act as an antiseptic. I tied it with my handkerchief, and bandaged it with the flour sack I had my bannock in. I figured my blood-soaked underwear would hold it all in place. The little fire was giving some heat and the blood hadn't frozen yet. I must have lost an hour there, but my leg was still functioning, so I thought I'd better run to save my dogs and keep from freezing my feet.

The sun went down as we crossed the Lake, and we travelled all night for about twelve hours on the river, following the trail which Pete and I had made two days before. It was about forty degrees below zero and brilliant moonlight, there was no wind and no sound except the occasional hoot-owl, and me swearing at the dogs.

The dogs were getting tired, even good dogs get tired if you're not a good dog driver, and I wasn't a good dog driver by a long way. After about ten miles on the river my knee was so stiff and hurting so badly that I had to ride on the toboggan. I rode standing on the tail of the toboggan until I thought my leg would freeze, then I crawled into my bedroll, but my foot wouldn't warm up, I kept pounding it with my whip handle to try and keep it from freezing.

71

I was hungry but I couldn't stop to make camp, there was no place to camp on the river, and I couldn't get up off the river, in any case, I was scared to stop, if I had I would never have made it. The dogs got tired and just crawled along, and it was long after daylight, and I was just about frozen stiff, when at last we made the baseline. The trail here went straight up off the river for about a hundred feet, up a fifty foot bank. The dogs were too tired, and it was too steep for them to pull me up, and I couldn't walk.

I never quit, there is always a way, I had a quarter-inch rope that had been used to fasten the load on my toboggan, I tied that to the end of the tail rope that was fastened to the head of the toboggan, together with any other bits of rope that I could find. Then I hung onto the end of the rope, sent the dogs to the top of the bank, and called them to stop.

They held the sleigh at the top of the bank while I pulled myself up the bank with the aid of the rope. It was sure some chore, for my leg was so badly frozen and so stiff, it was useless, but I was determined to get up that hill and I wiggled up somehow. Once on top I loaded myself onto the toboggan again. The snow was about three feet deep and there were two or three miles to go across the flat to the camp, but as soon as the dogs smelled the smoke from the cabins they forgot their weariness and we soon arrived at Magloire's cabin.

Magloire came out and helped me in, he looked after the dogs and the women went to work on me. They cut off my frozen clothes, my moccasins, and sock, even the flour sack was frozen, and they had to soak it in warm water to get it off. I told them to leave the soap, I didn't want my knee to start bleeding again. They washed it off as well as they could and got it fairly clean. The hole was all swollen, and still black inside but I figured it was just soot off the stick, so I told them to leave it. They had no disinfectant, so they bandaged it up with flour sacks using lard to stop them from sticking.

They made me something to eat and I sat in front of the fire in my mackinaw jacket, at last I was warm again! While I was sitting there, Narcise Capotblanc came in to see me.

"You're a hell of a man to tell us the trail to the lake was good, we couldn't find It." I told him. He laughed.

"It's a good trail, but it's been blowing so hard it's drifted over. We would have been over it but it's turned so cold." The women washed out my clothes, dried them, and sewed them up again where they'd had to cut them to get them off, and I went to sleep. Magloire woke me up when he was ready to leave, he had tied his toboggan on top of mine, and put his four dogs ahead of my four, I lay down on the toboggan in my bedroll, and let Magloire do all the work. We made the twenty-five miles home just before dark, where I went to bed and stayed there for two or three weeks.

My leg was so stiff I couldn't bend it to get it into a washtub to soak it for several days, then I soaked it every day for a couple of weeks, after which I could bend it a little. I tried to soak out the burnt wood but I never did get it all out, even when it healed you could still see the black stain under the skin for years. My frostbitten foot blistered here and there especially my big toe but it healed up too in time.

Pete returned after the hunters got back to Slavey Lake. Antoine Courtorielle, had killed a moose the first day after they'd left, so they had meat, but were glad they didn't have to make the long trip to the post to get grub, for they were still weak and played out easily. Pete had done well with his trade and brought back enough fur to cover all the supplies we had taken. Magloire told him of my accident, and what a wonder it was I had made it back to his camp.

"Not good to travel alone!" said Magloire.

CHAPTER SIXTEEN

The Story of John Brown

In 1925 John Brown came in early from the bush saying that fur was not as good as last year. He wanted to go to Peace River on the ice with the mailman Louis Bourassa, so I took him down to the river. John intended to sell his fur in Edmonton, and asked me to meet him when I was in town to settle up our business.

The hunters came in with varying degrees of success as usual, and I wound up my first season, I wouldn't know how well I had done until I sold the fur. Allie and his daughter Emma came in off the first boat, and we left them to look after things while Louise and I took the boys to Edmonton.

In the train, a woman who got on at one stop and sat close to us was very sick. A few days later Arthur was taken ill, Dr. Brander came right away from the clinic, which was only a block away from the King Edward, he took one look at Arthur and said,

"Diphtheria! Where did he pick that up?" We told him about the woman on the train, and Dr. Brander notified the health authorities. She was a big headache to them, for she visited friends before they picked her up and took her to hospital. Arthur went to hospital for two weeks, and Louis was inoculated with no ill effects.

Meanwhile I rounded up John Brown, who told me he wanted me to buy him out. This was quite a blow, and I told him I didn't think I could manage it. I went to Lamson and Hubbard and told them what John had said. As far as I could see my only choice was to pay John, and the wholesaler and go home and forget all about it.

"Don't do that," the manager said, "Let's see if we can work something out."

The returns for the fur were seven thousand, and I asked John what he wanted for his share. John was planning to go and trap northeast of Lake Athabasca next season, and he said he wanted two thousand in cash, plus he wanted me to buy his trapping outfit for him. He gave me a list of things he wanted packed, and shipped to Ft. McMurray by the end of August, they included an eighteen foot canoe with toboggan and harness.

I made up an agreement dissolving our partnership and showed it to John, he said he thought it was O.K. but we would find a lawyer and show it to him. We went to see the first one we found. John handed him the agreement and asked him if he would witness our signatures on it. The lawyer read the agreement and said,

"Have you received these goods shipped to Ft. McMurray?"

"No," said John, "But I will."

"Well then," said the lawyer, "You would be a fool to sign this." The wyer did his best to advise him, but John just said,

"Give me a pen, and witness our signatures." It was signed and settled, and John asked him how much he owed him.

"Ten dollars," was the reply.

"What," said John, "Just for witnessing our signatures?"

"No," said the lawyer, "For wasting my time arguing!" I said,

"John, pay him and let's go."

Mr. Pike, the Lamson and Hubbard manager suggested that I give John a thousand dollars cash, and an order for a thousand dollars on Lamson and Hubbard, payable this time next year. John agreed to this in order to help me, but I don't think he ever collected the second thousand dollars.

After I had settled up, made my requisition out, and signed an agreement for another year, I received a cheque for a thousand dollars which I deposited into an account with the Bank of Montreal. Believe me, it looked like a fortune in contrast to what I went through, and what I got out of shipping the cows previously.

Business finished, we set off for home. The boat was downriver and we would have four or five days to wait. Louis Paul, a trapper from the Fort who intended to trap out of Keg River the coming winter, was anxious to get going too, so we bought a small boat. We had nothing but suitcases to carry, Louis and I piloted in turns, and young Louis and Arthur were kept busy bailing which was good fun for them. We travelled nonstop, and reached the landing in two days.

All was well at home, I told Allie I would be trading again this year, and he said he thought I ought to open a post at the lake which was on the river trail fifteen miles before Slavey Lake. It had a Slavey name which I forget, but translated it meant Drowned Horse Lake. Pete and I had passed it on our way to Slavey Lake the previous winter. Isidore's outfit were moving down there and building cabins. Allie had had the news from Magloire, who also told him that he couldn't hay for me this year, but he said there was good hay on the Chinchaga, as it had been burnt off in the spring, that was good news.

Allie said that if I would like to open a post at the lake, he would run it for me this winter, as he had nothing to go back to Peace River for. Allie used to be a rich man at one time, owning a half interest in the Grande Prairie Lumber Co., as well as about half the Shaftesbury settlement, a hundred head of horses, a full line of machinery, and good buildings on the farm. I never found out what the trouble was, but the bank foreclosed and took everything, so Allie was anxious to do something to enable him to live.

"Allie, that will mean building a place down there."

"Yes, but one fair sized building will be enough, and Magloire says they are building in a bunch of dry spruce with logs easy to get; they only have to haul them a few hundred yards."

"It will mean a seventy or eighty mile trip with practically no road, we'll have to follow the Chinchaga for fourteen miles west, then there is only a pack trail. We'll see if we can get Magloire to widen out that trail for a wagon, but first I have to buy three good sleigh dogs for John."

As luck would have it, Napoleon Capotblanc came in from the lake to fetch his wife who had been staying on the prairie with her parents. He could speak a little English, having been at the Mission school. I told him our plans, and sent a message to Magloire to cut out the packtrail wide enough for a wagon. Napoleon also sold me a good dog for seventy-five dollars in trade at the new store. I managed to find two more good dogs, so now I was ready to take them to the river.

Dick Naylor was leaving Revillons, and going to Washington where he had friends. He agreed to take my dogs with him on the boat, and ship them to Brown from Edmonton. He did this and wired Brown when to expect them. I gave him my order on Lamson and Hubbard to cover the expense he would be put to, not forgetting to add the cost of a crock. Brown got his dogs safely, and Dick never did put in any account for this. I have always been grateful to Dick, but I never saw him again, and Clarence Rankin took over his post at Revillons.

When John received his dogs and equipment, he went to Fondulac on the northeast corner of Lake Athabasca, there was hardly anyone living there but John, the Hudson's Bay Agent, and the R.C.M.P. John trapped north of the post and didn't come back until the end of January. He had made a good hunt and the price agreed upon for the fur was $3,000, he and the agent were looking over the fur, when the R.C.M.P. officer came along and asked to see John's trapping licence. John showed it to him and said,

"Here you are it's alright." The officer looked at it and said,

"No it's not, it's an Alberta licence, and this is Saskatchewan. I'll have to seize the fur, and your trapping outfit." Which he did. John was left with his dog team, and all he could do was to head for Ft. McMurray over the ice with his dog team.

A book could have been written about John Brown's exploits. John was six feet tall, slim, quiet, with a thin face and medium brown hair. He was Polish, but spoke good educated English. John's father was a lawyer in Poland, and when he died he left John a share of the estate, but John wrote back to the lawyers in Poland, and told them to give his share to the poor!

John didn't smoke or drink, or wash, and he hardly spent any money. He stayed at our place once when the boys were small, and they got him water, soap, and a towel to wash. "Wash?" he said, "It'll rain soon." When his clothes got bad he threw them away and bought new ones. He wouldn't stay in the house, he slept in his bedroll outside, he just had one blanket for his bedroll. He never told us when he intended to leave, he just wasn't there!

John was a Catholic and very religious, I had to be careful what I said to him or I would set him off preaching. He never heard from his relatives, but he sent letters to me from time to time, he was a real loner, and never married, but I got on real well with him.

John just loved to wander, he was a self-taught trapper and trapped at the mouth of the Third Battle River on the Peace for quite a long time. He was always on the go, trapping all day and half the night, going round his traps with a lantern made out of a candle in a lard pall, skinning rats as he hurried from one trap to another.

John never packed grub, once on Lake Athabasca, the waves got so big his canoe was washed up on a sandbar which was covered with stranded fish, so he ate raw fish to keep alive. I've seen him eating wild ducks, he'd put them in front of the campfire, and when they were cooked through the hide he'd eat them. They'd still be raw inside and blood would run through his fingers as he ate. I didn't know much about him when I first met him of course, but I got to know him quite well over the years.

He went to Alaska to trap, and teamed up with a Swede named Nels, fur was plentfiul, he wrote, especially marten. John wanted to go to Siberia to trap, but they wouldn't let him in, all the trappers there were Government employed; John was a Canadian citizen, but it's a wonder he didn't go anyway, with or without permission. They were forty miles out of Fairbanks, and when his partner went into Fairbanks the police asked him about John. Nels told them he was a good trapper from the Peace River country, the Alaskan police wrote to the police in Peace River, who wrote to me, but John didn't wait around, when he heard the police had been asking about him.

"I'm not getting tangled up with the police anymore, I'm leaving right now, you can take up my traps." John told his partner.

John took five pounds of tea and two bannock, and pulled out. He walked from Fairbanks to Great Bear Lake where he hung around for most of the summer. Ray Ross was running the Hudson's Bay Post at that time and remembered him. Ray was sent to Keg River Post later, and he and his family became close friends of ours. When John reached Great Bear Lake he had one dog left, having eaten the other. He caught marten on the way, and carried out as much as he could carry.

He wrote to me and told me that he intended to trap down the Coppermine that winter. The next year I had a letter from John posted at Hearne Point in the Arctic. He said there wasn't much fur on the headwaters of the Coppermine so he had followed it down to the mouth at Hearne Point, where there was quite a settlement.

Spring came before he got there, and he had to walk as there were no trees to make a raft. The river bank was very rough, and part way down he ran into an old camp where there was a skeleton lying in bed in what had been a tent, though it was all rotten and blown to shreds, John informed the police who were stationed in the settlement, and agreed to take them back to it after freezeup the next fall.

Later I heard that he had bought an island in the mouth of the Coppermine River where he intended to raise white fox. He ordered wire and building materials from the Hudson's Bay to be sent via Vancouver, meanwhile he lived in a tent. Henry A. Larsen in his book The Big Ship*tells of transporting John Brown on his last journey from the Arctic. John is said to have threatened an Eskimo woman with his gun when she came near his island to lay out traps. John told me that the Hudson's Bay had sent her, and that she fired on him first, after which John said he fired shots over her head, and when the police came he said he showed them the holes in his tent where she had shot at him.

In any case, eighty white fox he had caught were confiscated to pay his expenses to Edmonton to undergo psychiatric examinations! The next I heard of him he was in the mental hospital at Ponoka. Talk to John about religion and he was crazy, but set him down in the bush, and he was harmless, and as crazy as hundreds of other trappers in the north. I visited him in Ponoka, and did what I could for him but eventually he died there.

---

*Published by McClelland and Stewart, 1967.

Louis, Louise, and Art at Keg River.

Freighting Through The Bush.

Revillon Frere's Trading Post at Keg River.

Trappers with their dog teams at Keg River Trading Post.

Freight arriving at Keg River Trading Post.

Hauling hay at Keg River in the winter.

Keg River Trading Post.

Peace River Railway Depot 1930 — Photo Peace River Centennial Museum.

CHAPTER SEVENTEEN

Fire On The Prairie

It was summertime and the men were busy haying, I had to leave them to it and go down to the river. That summer John Christian had built me a warehouse alongside Revillon's warehouse, and I went down to the river alone to warehouse my freight. It was getting late in the season, and I had a short wait at the landing until the boat came in, and the deckhands dumped my twelve tons of freight in the mud at the end of the gangplank. I dragged it out of the mud and by degrees carried it up to the warehouse, selected what we needed immediately, and left for home.

After I got to the top of the hill by the Keg Crossing, I saw smoke from some big fire out west. About ten miles further I saw the fire across the Keg to the south, with the wind blowing from that direction. After another three of four miles I found it coming up on this side of the Keg at a fair speed. I still had hay on the wagon for feeding at noon camp, and I dumped it in case I met the fire later and had to go through it.

I didn't get far before I came to the place where the main head of fire had just crossed the trail. I pounded through the fire for three miles. I was scared to stop as it was hard to tell if it was on the prairie or not. I made the prairie alright, but I could see it was all alight south of the Keg about a mile away.

I then met an Indian, with a white man by the name of McLeod, who had just come in from the Fort. The Indian had two stacks of hay down there and seeing the fire had come down to see if he could save his hay stacks. I told them to stay there and try and stop the fire from starting up the prairie, I would bring them help, grub, and water as soon as I could.

I still had six or seven miles to go to get home, with the smoke so thick I couldn't tell where the fire was. I never got back to those two men, they were there all day fighting the fire, but they saved the stacks. I was eating my supper after I got home, when someone came in to tell me that the fire was coming in from the west, this I knew could hit the prairie.

The house and garden were covered with ash as if it had been snowing. I got the men who were haying to take a wagon with barrels of water, and all the natives they could find to go out to the fire, and try and head it off. There was a wagon trail of sorts up the hill, for about five miles, where they could try and put out the side-fire, and I would try and get some more help, and be back as soon as I could. Before I left I had asked Louise to bake as much bannock as she could, as I knew I would have to feed the crew when I got out to the fire.

The men were all strung out fighting the side-fire, which was burning in small poplar and fairly easy to put out, some of the men went two or three miles south to see that the fire didn't swing out towards the prairie. When I got there, the fire was heading for a spruce bluff, it was out of the question to try and stop this head fire.

While all this was going on, I rounded up Trosky who was freighting for Revillons, he had two stacks of hay down at this end of the prairie, and I asked him if he would come out to the fire. He told me to look after my stacks and he would look after his.

Before leaving the fire I told one of the natives I would go back home and bring water and grub out and asked them to stay until I returned. When I got back the men were congregated at the spruce bluff which was then alight. We ate bannock and drank tea, and some wanted to go home. I encouraged them to stay awhile to make sure that the fire didn't start up again on the west side, they were satisfied to stay as long as the tea and bannock lasted. During the night or early morning the wind sprang up from the south blowing quite strongly, it took the fire out of the spruce and roaring straight north, so just before daylight we left for home.

On getting back to the prairie we saw what Trosky had done to protect his stacks. He had plowed five or six furrows around the stacks, left about twenty-five feet, then plowed another five or six furrows around that, then he had burnt the grass in between the two lanes of plowing. Then I suppose he just left it, when we passed by, the fire had crawled under the plowing and set the stacks on fire, crawled out on the outside of the plowing and burnt up one of my stacks. Luckily the fire went out by itself, but I lost about thirty tons of hay.

It was too late to cut any more if we could find it, as it was frozen too much. Magloire knew of a big slough near the Chinchaga where he thought we could hay. This would mean a nine mile haul after freezeup, to get it home over the swamp, but I told Pete to go and see what it was like, though probably the fire had got it all. There was plenty of slough grass that wasn't too frozen but it was impossible to get at because of windfall willows, it was too bad, in that case, that the fire didn't get down there, it would have cleaned them all up.

CHAPTER EIGHTEEN

Cattle Trading

On his way back to the Fort, Pete looked at Buffalo Prairie and found plenty of hay there, so I sold him thirty head of cattle, he would trail them after New Year's when the ice was solid on the river. He made a deal with one of the natives to haul two loads of hay down to the Peace so that he would have night-feed for the cows. I had made a baler, so I sent a load of baled hay to the Keg Crossing for the first night, it was the only way to haul hay over that trail. The second night they would spend at Dick McGranes, the third night they should reach Buffalo Prairie. Pete trailed them successfully, they wintered well, and some calved.

Stub Lapp was trading for Sheridan Lawrence at Hay Lakes. The place where they had their warehouses, between Ft. Vermilion and Hay Lakes Stub called High Level, for it was the only dry spot in that area, this is where the town of High Level stands today. Stub rode over on a saddle horse he had bought, and stayed with us; during our conversation he said he wished he had some cows, as he always had a lot of hay for the horses, and he might as well raise some beef. He accepted my offer of twenty head of she stock and a bull for a thousand dollars. I told him I would take a credit order on Sheridan Lawrence for flour and pork to pay for them, and agreed to deliver them free if he would grubstake the men to come back.

We brought the cows in and sorted out the ones to take to Stub Lapp. I decided to pack the bull, I put a pack-saddle on him, loaded him up and tried to move him, he gave a grunt and set off without further complaint, he was as gentle as a hound pup. It took us three days to reach Rainbow. Allie was sure surprised to see me arrive with the cows, we found Magloire at home for it was too early to trap much. Magloire agreed to take the cows to Hay Lakes and would get Jean Cardinal to go with him. He figured it would take three days going and two coming back, so I grubstaked them and gave Magloire twenty-five dollars and Jean Cardinal ten dollars, Stub would grubstake them coming back.

The cattle arrived safely, but unfortunately Stub Lapp's venture into the cattle business ended in disaster for he failed to put up enough hay for them, so shot them and sold the meat to the Slaveys for dog meat.

Meanwhile I sent a letter to Sheridan Lawrence telling him about my deal with Stub Lapp, he replied telling me that as Stub Lapp owed him money the cattle were really his, but he would send me the flour and pork that I wanted. Sheridan eventually sent the pork, it was some pork there wasn't a pailful of lard on the whole works. Apparently the small pigs had developed rheumatism and Sheridan had butchered about a hundred of them. I split them in half and sold them all in spite of being so thin; I could have sold more, for fresh pork was a rarity.

I got mixed up in another cattle deal with Narcise Capotblanc of all people. When he came in from Rainbow, I asked him why he hadn't paid his debt to me, for I knew he had made a good hunt.

"Fred Paul came over to Rainbow on a visit and told us we could get higher prices for our fur at the Fort, and would be paid in cash."

"Did you do this Narcise?" I asked him.

"No, I went home with Fred, and he talked me into buying twelve head of cattle, and took all my fur to pay for them."

"What are you going to do with the cattle Narcise?" I asked him.

"I don't know," he said.

"Did you see them?" I asked.

"No, Fred's kids had turned them loose as they had used up all their hay, and they will have to rustle for themselves in the snow." Narcise figured I would have allowed him three hundred dollars on his fur.

"As the cattle are no good to you," I told him, "I will take them this fall, and allow you three hundred on your debt." I wrote out an order to Fred Paul for the cows, and got Narcise to sign it.

I took Pete with me to fetch the cattle; we went without packhorses or bedrolls and made Sheridan's place the second night. Sheridan said that Fred Paul's cows were so wild we would need help to get them out, so he sent two men with us.

We all left early in the morning, found the cattle and started to chase them through the bush, we lost them and found them again; we chased them all day without success. I was sure we could play them out, but no, in fact we chased them for three days, until I finally gave up in disgust. We might just as well have tried to corral moose! I asked the men to tell Sheridan what had happened, and ask him to shoot them for me and send the meat in the winter when he sent the flour.

Sheridan did shoot them and sent the meat, all forty-eight quarters, they were just skin and bone, they couldn't have been any thinner lf they'd tried. They were a scrub lot to start with, and leaving them so late in the winter didn't improve them. The meat looked like poor dog feed, Allie took some and said it would make good soup. I sent some to Rainbow and they howled about the price, but they had cost me a lot of money. I had to pay freight and pay the men that helped me chase them for three days! What a way to collect a three hundred dollar debt!

CHAPTER NINETEEN

Cutting a Trail to Rainbow Lake

Fred thought we could get enough hay at the Chinchaga but the ground was too rough to use the hayrack. Fred and his boys went down with the haying machinery to make a camp and clean up the dead willows. When Louis and Art heard of all this, they wanted to go too. I thought with all those boys camped on the riverbank, and only two or three feet of water in the river, the boys would have a whale of a time with not much work done. However, Fred made them pick up sticks in the morning before they could go swimming.

Allie and I had to pass the hay camp on our way to the lake to build our trading post, so we stopped and had a meal with them. The hay camp was up on the bank, there was only a packtrail on land, so we travelled on the river bottom. This wasn't bad travelling, but slow. When we got to the twenty-seventh baseline, we had to quit the river and get up on the bank as the water got too deep and there were quicksands instead of gravel. We had to widen the packtrail to get our wagon through, this was no great chore as it was only small poplar. While we were doing this who should come along but Louis Paul, the trapper who had come downriver with me in the skiff.

Louis was building a cabin about a mile from there on a little prairie where he was planning to trap that winter, as there were plenty of fox signs. He helped us cut the trail to his half-finished cabin where we stopped to eat and feed the horses. Louis seemed to be living on a diet of moosemeat with no bannock so I gave him fifty pounds of flour. He said he would come with us and help widen the trail and build our post, this suited us fine, so he threw the rest of his moosemeat in the wagon.

We had to cross the river here. The bank was a twenty or thirty foot drop, just about straight up and down. We had only one chain, so we ran a rail through the backwheels and under the wagon box, this arrangement seemed to be O.K. but the wagon box was not heavy enough to hold it. The hind end was thrown up in the air and over one wheel scattering half our load all over the riverbank, Louis' moosemeat flew out into the sand. As Louis said sand was better than flies, we could wash it off. This was my fault, I should have taken our chain and chained the box to the running gear, one is always learning!

We had about a mile of good going on the river bottom with only two or three feet of water, then we got up on the bank and started widening the trail. We made about a mile when we had to cross a small creek. I tried this on foot and nearly got bogged down, so unhitched the team and took them across, they almost got bogged down too, but we made it. I put a chain onto the end of the pole to pull the wagon across, but in the middle of the creek the wagon stuck, almost out of sight. As we would have to unload everything we decided to camp for the night. We had to make smudges, the mosquitoes were so bad. There was plenty of feed for the horses but they stayed close to the smudges. After supper we unloaded everything and packed it up in the bank, intending to pull the wagon out in the morning. We went to bed under our mosquito nets and believe me we couldn't see through those nets for insects.

We had a big struggle the next morning to get our wagon out. It was a terrible place, on a bend in a regular mudhole, but it was the only place to cross, the other places were too narrow and too deep. We jerked the wagon this way and that and put rails under it and eventually we got it out, reloaded it, and hit the trail. Allie drove, and Louis and I cut the trail for three or four miles, then we got held up by big windfall poplar which had to be moved with the team.

All the time I was expecting to meet Magloire, I wondered if he hadn't got my message. We made some headway, and then came to some windfall spruce, Louis Paul said it was not far to the native's cabins so we decided to have dinner. We were travelling along the south shore of the lake, it was only two or three hundred yards to get water, so we made camp. Allie was the cook and I took the team down to the water, and had to feed them the last of our hay, as there was no grass for them close by.

While we were eating Magloire and Peter Bottle came into camp, they had seen our smoke so came to see who it was. They were sawing on the other side of the windfall, Magloire was making logs twenty-five feet and twenty feet long that we could use for our building. We left the wagon in camp as we couldn't take it any further until the logs were snaked.

Louis and I snaked logs, Magloire and Pete cleared the trail and Allie stayed in camp to clean up the meat and cook. Antoine Bottle and Acquenezi came to help build the cabin and I had to feed them so it was a good job Louis brought that moosemeat. Allie took up flour to one of the native women and got her to make bannock. There were about eight or nine cabins built and occupied.

We cleared off a place for the building on the back of the lake about ten feet above high water. Magloire and Pete finished clearing the trail, then they helped us with the building, Magloire and a helper went for roof rails, and two men cut rushes for the roof as there was no spruce bark available.

Acquenezi asked me if I would like some fish and I said, sure. After supper that night we took a packhorse to a creek that ran out of the lake, where Acquenezi had built a fish trap of willows. It was full of fish and we brought two panniersful back to camp. We had over a hundred pounds, they were about eight inches long, quite round, and as full of bones as they could get! To my notion all they were good for was dog feed.

I intended leaving early the next day leaving Magloire to hew poplar for the door, chink the building, and put dirt on the roof. This is satisfactory for the winter, as you can brush the snow off, but in the summer it rains inside the building for half a day after it's stopped raining outside.

We didn't get away as early as we had hoped as it was raining, but it cleared up by noon. A huge rainbow came up out of the lake in the east, arched over to the west and went back into the lake. It was brilliant. I said to Allie who was admiring it,

"Rainbow Lake! That would be a good name for the lake." It has been called Rainbow Lake ever since. This neck of the woods is now the Rainbow Lake oilfields, and Rainbow Lake town is northwest of the original Rainbow Lake settlement.

Old Emilieu Bottle hadn't settled up for the team Allie had sold him two years ago, so Allie was going to take it back. Emilieu didn't ride them because he was scared to death of them, they weighed fourteen or fifteen hundred pounds and were full of life, after riding small cayuses all his life, no wonder he was scared of those two.

The other horses Allie left here died of swamp fever. It took a big horse to carry Allie, but the team he got back from Emilieu were too much for him to handle. So I bought them from him. I took them down to the hay camp, but Fred would have nothing to do with them, he said that if he put the lines down for a minute they would run away, so I gave Allie one of the cayuses to try out. Allie came back next morning saying his troubles were over. He had traded the cayuse, plus twenty dollars that I was to give him in trade from the store, to Maurice Desjarlais for a buckskin horse he'd brought from Notikewin. This horse carried Allie well.

Allie and I hauled hay and baled it for freighting, we went to the river to meet the boat, and warehouse the freight, bringing back as much as we could haul. Alphonse Bottle was in to meet Revillon's freight, and as it didn't arrive, he helped us. Jean Marie Cardinal, a native boy from the Sucker Creek Reserve on Lesser Slave Lake, came in on the boat, he spoke good English and was on his way to stay with Isidore Capotblanc. I agreed to take him out to Rainbow, if he would help us pack freight which he did, this was a big help as there was around thirty tons of freight to pack up to the warehouse.

Once home, Allie wanted to go right away to Rainbow Lake. The ground was not frozen so he would have to take a packteam, I had only one packsaddle with panniers, but I borrowed three, and Allie set to work to make two more out of cow hides I had in the warehouse from some of my cows that had died. I had to make two saddles, Allie came up with a handful of iron rings and I used gunny sacks for cinches. This made six outfits.

Allie had his buckskin mare to ride, I rode my saddlehorse and we had a cayuse for Jean Cardinal to ride. There was good pasture for packhorses at the lake, you could see them a mile away feeding up on the hillside south of the lake. We got our packs together allowing a hundred pounds for each load, and made Rainbow Lake in two days. I came back alone chasing the horses, I had trouble keeping up with them so I didn't camp overnight.

Later Pete and Emma went down with team and sleighs. I shod the team as they expected to run into some smooth ice on the Chin. The team weren't at all fussy about being shod, but they made a good working team, with freight and hay they had quite a load. They had some trouble on the river at Louis Paul's cabin, the ice wasn't strong enough, and he had to unload everything twice, to get the sleighs out of the river. There was only a foot of water but quicksands underneath. He noticed that Louis Paul had some log pens with fox in them, probably feeding them until their coats got prime.

Allie sent back a requisition, it was quite a job making this up as I had to invoice it all based on the trading price. John Christian took this back, and managed without incident. Allie sent back fox, mink and rats. As the winter progressed the snow got deep, and an everlasting wind blew it into drifts.

John said there would be too much snow to haul to Rainbow, but Allie had sent another requisition so I would have to send one more load. Pete was the only one who could handle Allie's team with all that snow, and it took a good team, so I managed to get him to go, and sent a message to Allie not to order any more than he actually needed as the snow was getting too deep.

It seemed to me that the squirrels should be of some value, so I thought I would buy some and take them to Edmonton and find out. I bought them from the kids, they were very plentiful some in every spruce tree and easily caught with a snare. I bought a thousand or more of these and took a hundred into Edmonton to see what I could do with them. I couldn't find any of the dealers that knew what they were, but Louis Lawes, agent for Winnipeg Fur Auctions sent some to Winnipeg to see what the manufacturers thought of them and they sold them for 25¢.

By now we had radio, and the radio station in Edmonton spent half its broadcasting time sending out messages to people in the north. We used to listen at one o'clock each day. Friends and relatives of Hudson's Bay Managers would send them letters to the radio station and they would be read out on the air. An Englishman did the job for years, and he must have had an awful thirst, for he used to stop and say,

"Just a minute, I must have a drink." And you could hear him pour it out and drink it.

At two o'clock every Wednesday Louis Lawes the Winnipeg Fur Auction Agent had the fur prices broadcast in a coded message, so I was kept well informed about fur prices, the market was holding at a good level for the present.

In the spring Pete brought Emma back from Rainbow with a load of fur together with Louis Paul who had made a good hunt, then Pete took Louis to the Fort with his dogs before the snow got too soft, to catch the first boat.

Louis sold his fur in Edmonton and he was walking down the street with about three thousand dollars in his pocket when he was rolled, and his cash taken from him. Louis was so mad he attacked the man and half killed him, as a result he was arrested and committed to the mental hospital at Ponoka. About two years later he escaped, and walked all the way to Keg River without touching a road. He called in to tell us about it, his hair and beard were long, we hardly knew him, then he left to continue north.

"Where are you going?" I asked him.

"Where no-one can find me." he replied.

CHAPTER TWENTY

Trading at Rainbow and Tangling With The Bay

The next fall Allie went down to Rainbow with a packhorse team as before and Emma went down later with sleighs when the ground froze. Later I sent John down with a load of flour and he came back with a message from Allie. It seemed that Slavey Indians from Zama Lake had asked Allie to go and trade over there, for their nearest post was at Hay Lakes.

Magloire widened out the trail, I bought a building, took freight over by sleighs and Allie traded there for two years. He showed a loss both winters. Mr. Stanton the Revillon Freres District Manager at Hay River told me that as the Hudson's Bay company intended to go into Zama Lake, Revillons intended to go in too. I told him that the best thing they could do was to take over my place together with the inventory, and I would quit. They did this, and installed Allie as manager. Allie ran it for two winters and then they closed it down when fur got so short.

Meanwhile McLeod, the butter-maker from Peace River, originally from Ontario, traded for me at Rainbow. McLeod did a fair job the first winter, although we found that getting hay for the teams was quite a problem. There was a good hay meadow on the west end of the lake where a man could get a hundred of hay if he wanted, so I decided to take a mower and rake down there.

Harry Bowe had killed off the few cows he had and was going to trap that winter, he had no use for his mower and rake, so I bought it from him. I told Acquenezi I would bring them down on a raft at high water, and tie them up at the landing where the trail to Rainbow left the river. I told him they could use them if they would put up one stack for me. They did this which gave me plenty of hay for the freight teams.

Hauling the mower and rake was quite an adventure. I made a raft at the Chin, loaded the mower and rake aboard and rafted down to Rainbow Lake landing which was about a hundred miles. The river was booming full and we travelled at a fair speed. Sweepers were quite a hazard, these are spruce trees which have fallen but are still attached by their roots, and sticking out in the river. I managed to miss one lot, only to get stuck on another bunch with a sweeper between two of the raft logs. This happened about thirty or forty feet from the edge of the bank.

The front of the raft was down in the water, and the mower was in danger of sliding into the river, so I had to move it back. I had a twelve foot pole to steer the raft and I juggled and juggled but I couldn't get the sweeper off. It sure had me guessing, I was there half a day struggling with it, I finally levered it off using an axe and a rope.

The river is full of bends with long narrow points. I stopped and had lunch with Hume Stewart who had a cabin on the neck of one of these points, then I travelled the twenty-three miles around the point, tied up the raft and walked over the neck of the point, back to Hume's place for supper. It took me two days to get to the landing, I tied up the raft as arranged, and walked back home to the Keg, about seventy miles or so. That took me about a day, once I start walking, I never stop.

On the way back I spent some time watching a white muskrat with her family of five little white rats about two inches long swimming up the river. Later I bought quite a few white rats from a trapper that had caught them at Slavey Lake west of Keg River. A river running out of this lake emptied into the Chin not far above where I saw the old rat and the little ones.

I didn't buy beaver that spring as it was closed season. Fur prices were falling, Louis Lawes broadcast that there was quite a slump in the spring market sales, and to be careful how I bought. That didn't help as we had already bought for the season, however, we had to make the best of things, maybe there would be an improvement in the next sales.

I think it was the summer of 1929 that Fred Clark, Joe Kemp's brother-in-law, and the New Hudson's Bay manager came down to see me with a summons for the account that I owed Lamson and Hubbard in Edmonton, telling me that he had been authorized to collect it. It seemed that the Hudson's Bay had bought out Lamson and Hubbard and notified Fred to collect this account from me. This was a bit of a shock, I asked him for the bills, he said he hadn't any, so I told him to leave as I didn't intend to pay anything without the bills.

I wrote to Mr. Ben Spencer, manager for a wholesale dry goods house and a man I much admired, asking him to find out from Mr. Pike the manager of Lamson and Hubbard if they had really disposed of their holdings. I sent Mr. Spencer a cheque on the Bank of Montreal to pay for incidental expenses, I had a little over a thousand dollars in it at that time.

He wrote back to tell me that the trusteeship of my account had been turned over to the Hudson's Bay, and they had put a garnishee on my account with the Bank of Montreal. My account with Mr. Pike was not due until July, and I wrote to say that I would pay it then.

When I went to Edmonton to see Ben Spencer, he had a cheque for me from the Winnipeg Fur Auctions, though all the fur wasn't sold as yet. I took the cheque over to the Union Bank and opened an account with it. Then I went to the Hudson's Bay office to see what I could do. According to my books I thought I owed them about eighteen hundred dollars.

The manager told me he couldn't find any account in my name or the Keg River Trading Post. I went back the next day, and they still hadn't found it, they said there was nothing in Lamson and Hubbard's books about my account and I told them they were nuts. What right had they to garnishee my account at the Bank of Montreal for non-payment of a non-existent account!

They said they must have it somewhere, I told them to find it, and meanwhile to remove the garnishee. They said they couldn't do that, so I told them I would go and see a lawyer to find out if they could garnishee my account for non-payment of a bill they couldn't produce! The next day they still couldn't find anything, so I said I would start proceedings against them. That will cost money, they said, and they would certainly find my account in time, and how much did I think I owed them? I said about a thousand or a little more. Give us a thousand on account, they said and we'll remove the garnishee. That didn't suit me, I told them the only way I would give them the thousand, was in settlement of the account in full.

They agreed to do this and our lawyers sorted out the details. Ray (my lawyer) thought I was a damn fool, but I told him it was better this way, it would have cost money to sue them, and this way we were ahead of the game. I gave him fifty dollars and he told me to go home and raise cows, and not to do anything like that again, it just wasn't business! Later that summer and in following years, Mr. Bartleman, the Hudson's Bay manager sent me a season's pass on the Hudson's Bay boats.

I told Ben Spencer I would be back later to order my freight, when all my fur returns would in. I still hadn't been paid for two grizzly bears, two hundred weasels, and two thousand squirrels. As it happened there was a slump in the market and the Winnipeg Fur Auctions went bankrupt. They had advanced money on fur, and when the market slumped they didn't get paid as much as they'd paid out, so I never did get paid for that fur.

The following year fur was still scarce and the trappers weren't satisfied with the prices, squirrels went down to 20¢, and skunk were worthless. The market continued to drop and some lines were impossible to sell at all. I took my fur to Martin Wener in Peace River who was buying for the Western Hide and Fur Company in Edmonton. I had thousands of squirrels but not much else.

About this time I started to trade with the wholesalers in Peace River, Marshall Wells, and Horne and Pitfield, which was a big saving in interest, though I still got my dry goods from Ben Spencer. A right of way was being cut for the Dominion Government Telegraph, and I figured that if I ran short of freight, I could come out with teams and sleighs in the winter.

Louis Bourassa came in on the boat about 1930 bringing a wagon, team and sleighs; he took up a homestead, built a house and barn on it, then he made a deal with the Hudson's Bay Post to build a post at Rainbow Lake right alongside mine, and he would run it for them the following winter. There was nothing I could do to stop them, even when they would be using the road which I had gone to the expense of cutting; they played the same trick at Zama Lake.

CHAPTER TWENTY-ONE

A Scatteration of Garbage Cans

On one trip to Edmonton I met Sheridan Lawrence, he was also on his way to Edmonton. He had twelve steers on board, and was taking them to Peace River to sell to the butcher. They were big shorthorns, four years old, weighing fourteen or fifteen hundred pounds.

I was staying at the Royal Hotel while waiting for the Edmonton train. Vern McLean and A. J. Bryson were there too, they were still ranching at Ft. St. John and we were catching up on our news when Jack McKinnon came in. He wanted us to take Sheridan's steers to the butcher's farm up the hill about four miles west. Bryson was leaving right away with horses but McLean had to take freight by boat and wasn't leaving yet, so McKinnon persuaded us to go. He borrowed two saddle-horses from another livery barn and bought us coveralls to protect our clothes.

Vern was an all-round cowboy, he couldn't be beat, he got on his horse and said,

"We'll see if these horses are any good." His horse bucked all over the place and so did mine, then he wanted to run away. We were behind the Peace Hotel, and there was a gap in the fence. I suppose there had been a gate, but it was now missing, behind the fence they kept their garbage cans. My horse headed for that gap and bucked around in there. Garbage cans and their contents were flying all over. It was lots of fun while it lasted, half the town came out to watch; there was sure a scatteration of garbage cans. However, I got my horse quietened down eventually.

We went down to the boat and told the deckhands to turn the steers loose. The steers were huge, they were bigger than our horses! It was like turning a cyclone loose, and they just hit for the bush. All that part of town was heavy poplar and we lost two of them in it, however, we managed to get ten in a bunch and decided to get them up to the farm.

We came back for the other two and tried and tried to herd them but with no success, so finally we roped them. Vern caught his up in the freight yard and tied him up to a box car! I tied mine to a tree where the Traveller's Motel is today. We took our horses back to McKinnon, told him what we had done and advised him to get them to the slaughterhouse right away as they might want to move that freight car!

Vern and I went back to the hotel for a well-earned drink. But that wasn't the end of it, McKinnon came again that evening to say that they'd got the steer that was tied to the box car but hadn't been able to get the other one as he was too wild. Would we come down in the morning and give the boys a hand to take it down to the slaughterhouse. Vern said he was leaving at daylight for Fairview, and I said I was leaving on the train for Edmonton. McKinnon said,

"That's good, I'll come and get you first thing in the morning, the train doesn't leave until three or four, you'll have plenty of time."

There seemed to be no escape, so I told him to bring his two men and a dray and I would see what I could do. I got the men to back the dray up to the tree, and crawling under it I put a chain around the steer's neck and tied it to the axle of the dray. That steer fought all the way to the slaughterhouse, pulling the team all over the country before we got there.

The slaughterhouse was just under the railroad bridge on Pat's Creek and the undertaker, who was a relation of the butcher and did the slaughtering for him, was waiting for us. I got the men to back the team up to the front door. The whole building was only about twenty feet square, built of upright poles with the butts in the ground.

I took the rope that was around the steer's horns under the door, then round one of the poles, the boards of the building didn't go to the ground so I had lots of room for this, then I put one of the men to pull up on this rope, to pull all he could.

The steer just stood there and made no attempt to go in the door, so I told the man I would entice the steer in and run out of the back door and slam it shut behind me, I told them to shut the door as soon as the steer was inside. It worked! The steer took off after me as I ran through the building, and I slammed the back door in its face.

Unfortunately, in the excitement, the undertaker got shut inside the building with the steer! The undertaker let out a yell, and the man I told to pull on the rope let it go and ran around to the front of the building to see what had happened. When I got to where the rope was supposed to be, there was no rope!

The steer had it all twisted round inside and took off after the undertaker, who climbed into the tank where they scalded the pigs. Behind the tank there was a ladder up to some device that they used to winch up the animals, the undertaker climbed this and yelled for us to tie up the steer. The undertaker was lying full length along the rafters and the steer had its front feet in the hog scalder he could just touch the undertaker with his nose, and he stood there blowing snot all over him!

I was still trying to get hold of the rope and I told the undertaker to shut up and keep still, or I would be the undertaker! Finally I got hold of the rope and got the men to help me pull it tight, then I had the steer's head tight up against the post. I went to the front door and opened it, telling the undertaker to come down. He said,

"Are you sure that animal can't get loose?" I told him it was quite safe and asked him how it happened.

"That damn fool pushed me in and shut the door," he said.

"I was supposed to shut the door, and when you came up to the door, I thought you wanted to go in, so I pushed you in so that I could shut the door," the man said.

What a lot of excitement for a few minutes! Fortunately no-one was hurt. I took the dray back to McKinnon and told him not to butcher the steer until the next day, if it didn't cool down first it would be as tough as an old boot!

I just had time to collect my grip and catch the train. On the train I asked Sheridan why he hadn't shipped the steers.to Edmonton. He said he'd got a good deal, sixty dollars each, clear of charges. At least he should have done, actually he got five hundred down and the balance later, and I don't think he ever did get the balance on those steers.

CHAPTER TWENTY-TWO

Freighting —
A Candle In The Grub Box

There was practically no hay left on the Keg, and the natives were having a hard time getting enough for their horses. We managed to get quite a bit from the head of the Paddle Creek, in and out between the willows, but this all had to be forked by hand as it was in small patches with too many dead sticks in the way.

I used to borrow Revillon's plow to plow my garden, and I was seriously thinking of breaking up some Government land with it this spring and planting a few acres of oats, for I was badly in need of them for the freight horses.

Everything had to be freighted in, thirty or forty trips a year were made either by me or hired help. Of these only about five or six trips were made in the summer, for then there was too much mud. The trail from the river went through sloughs and swamps which never dried up, even in summer. In the winter I could make the round trip in three days but the freighters I hired always took four days as they would never travel after dark. It took us a day longer to make the trip in the summer. If the snow got too deep in the winter we didn't go; the other freighters waited if they could, until I'd broken out the trail!

We needed two teams along to double up on the hills and get through the bogholes. It was hard on the sleighs, they were always breaking up on hidden stumps. I bought new sleighs almost every winter.

I used to pay a dollar and a half for a hundred pounds of freight hauled before freezeup and a dollar per hundred after freezeup. This made a ten or twelve dollar wage for man and team for four days hard work, different from today's pay, but I don't think anyone would do that job today for any money.

I set out in the winter whatever the temperature, forty, fifty or sixty below, but I was always properly dressed and prepared to make a good camp. I wore winter underwear of course, a shirt, and bib overalls. Bib overalls are easy to slip off in camp and dry out in a hurry if they get wet. If it was very cold I might wear a sweater and a moose hide jacket. I wore several thin layers on my hands and feet for the same reason, they could be separated and dried quickly if they got wet. On the outside I wore moose-hide mitts and moccasins on my hands and feet. On my head I wore an old sealskin cap jammed down, I don't know where I got it, but I wore it for years and years.

Before we set out Louise or I got the grub box ready. We boiled beans and potatoes and froze them into rounds like hamburger, the same with meat,

99

ground it and froze it, then packed in a gunny sack they were all ready to fry when we got to camp.

If we shot a partridge on the trail, we skinned it, cleaned it, opened it down the back and put it on a stick in front of the fire and roasted it. We always carried bannock of course. We also carried a frypan, a proper Hudson's Bay copper teakettle, a butcher knife, spoons, aluminum plates, and tea mugs. When I travelled alone I ate my meal straight out of the frypan, then if it froze before I'd finished I could put it back on the fire for a minute.

I always carried a candle in the grub box and matches in a little tin. I had birchbark and dry kindling in my pocket, birchbark isn't enough by itself for it flares up too quickly. We camped where there was good firewood, under spruce, or dry poplar, and as soon as we stopped we made fire. When making fire in the middle of the snow in extremely cold weather, the first thing to remember is to keep your mitts on, then with a scoop shovel, shovel the snow away leaving four or five inches above the moss. When the fire gets going, it only takes a minute for that to melt, soaking down, it wets the moss and prevents ground fires.

Crumple up dry sticks and kindling, and when it's all ready, take off one mitt and light the candle, slide it under the kindling, stick it in the snow and put your mitt back on right away, otherwise your hand will freeze, your mitt get cold, and if anything goes wrong, it's hard to warm up again. When the kindling gets going feed it dry sticks and slide your hand in and take the candle out, snuff it, and put it back in the grub box. When the fire is going well, which takes about five minutes, then you can take your mitts off and get to work.

We'd unhitch the team and blanket them over the harness, this keeps the blanket from touching the horses back, and if it snows the snow doesn't melt and can be brushed off. It also keeps the harness from freezing, if the harness is soaked with sweat and then allowed to freeze, then in the morning when you go to put it on it will crack. The next job is to feed the horses and get a meal ready.

If the wind was blowing at the back of us we'd put up a tarp to reflect the camp fire on the tarp, and keep us good and warm. We might put spruce boughs or willows down to keep our moccasins dry where the fire melted the snow, for it was important to keep our feet as dry as possible. My bedroll was made out of wavey down, which Allie bought for me at Hay Lakes. I made it with feather ticking, sewed into four inch tubes on the sewing machine, and stuffed with down. I had a tarp outside, and a bed blanket inside which could be washed.

The whole thing was about ninety inches square. I could get into that bedroll and cover my head and I didn't need a fire! The vapour from my breath would freeze around the edges. I used it for years until it died one night in Osborne's yard, but that is another story.

When we were all ready to go in the morning, but not before, we would put out the fire with snow. All the fires we lit when freighting, we never let one get away.

There was a steep hill up from the warehouse, it was a mile long and just wide enough for one wagon, and a thousand pounds was a good four-horse load. When the men were out on the traplines I did the hauling myself, and while the horses were feeding at the warehouse I would pack freight up the hill. Before I raised pigs, I bought sowbelly pork, which came in sacks weighing from a hundred and fifty up. It was easy to handle as it would lie on my back, and I could pack up three or four hundred pounds while the horses were eating.

On one trip the hill was so icy it took me all night to get my team and sleighs up the hill. The teams weren't shod which didn't help, and they couldn't stand, I couldn't stand either, or I would have packed the load up the hill myself. My sleigh ended up in the bush before I managed to get the load and team to the top of the hill.

I was freighting with John Christian once when we noticed sleighs and freight scattered all the way down to the bottom of the coulee. We found out that Mr. Rankin who was hauling for the Hudson's Bay, had been pulling the hill with a single team, when his team slipped back and over the side of the hill taking sleighs, team, and Mr. Rankin down the coulee. Charlie Rankin who was coming behind with the second load got his Dad out of the mess, and took him home where he died of internal injuries. It was really foolish to try and pull that hill with a single team. There was nothing we could do to help, so we loaded up our freight and went home. After this I went down with a slip, and spent a day widening out the hill to make it safer.

Up here you can never tell what the weather is going to do, whatever time of year it is. Frank Ferguson, Allie and I went to the river for freight one August. We were late for the boat and they had piled the cases in the mud with the sacked stuff on top, the weight had pushed the cases almost out of sight. We dragged everything out of the mud and up to the warehouse, and loaded up our two wagons.

We pulled one load up with the two teams, and camped for the night. The next morning we pulled the hill with the other load, and made the Keg Crossing by dark. After supper it started to rain, and I asked Frank if he was going to pull the Keg Crossing hill that night. He said, no, but told me to go ahead if I wanted to.

When I got to the top of the hill, it was really raining hard, so I decided to keep on going, it wasn't long before the rain turned to snow. I didn't stop until I got home, but it was five days before Frank and Allie arrived, they were mad because I had left them, but I reminded them that they had said they could manage, they had only themselves to blame. We had a foot of snow that storm, but it all went in a day or so.

In Edmonton I had asked the postal authorities for a Post Office at Carcajou, they agreed and I notified them that Mrs. Rankin would look after it. The Post Office was installed in her house at this side of the river. Mrs. Rankin went out to visit her relatives in Saskatchewan and her daughter-in-law, another Mrs. Rankin looked after the correspondence with the Edmonton office, and when old Mrs. Rankin returned, her daughter-in-law took the Post Office with her across the river where Charlie had his homestead. This was inconvenient for us, so eventually the postal authorities agreed to give us a mail service at Keg River. Revillons would look after it and, if I could find someone to haul the mail they would pay ten dollars a trip.

I got Harry Bowe to do it, and he did it for years, it meant three days work, an eighty mile trip for man and team for ten dollars! The mail came to Carcajou on the boat in the summer, and Harry hauled it to the Keg. In the winter Louis Bourassa hauled it on the ice, and Harry still hauled it from

Carcajou. Later on it came in by plane which landed at Keg River, and Harry hauled mail from Keg River to Carcajou.

One winter I decided to take McLeod and the freight down to Rainbow myself. I reshod the team, and put a freight-rack on the sleigh which stuck out about a foot on each side. We loaded it up with freight, hay, grub box, and bedrolls, and set off. We used to travel for a long way on the Chinchaga River below the hay camp and along the sandbar. There wasn't much snow, but I expected all kinds of glare ice. There was open water in several places, but ice under the cutbank, I decided that that was the best place to go, I guessed wrong!

We crowded as close to the cutbank as we could but suddenly without warning, the ice broke and the sleigh sank. The freighttrack floated, our bedrolls were on top, and we grabbed them and threw them onto solid ice as we jumped for shore ourselves. I jumped right back onto the freighttrack, and reached down into the water to get the drawpin out of the double trees, which freed the team.

They were standing in about ten feet of water, but I managed to get them onto the ledge under the cutbank without too much difficulty. Then I had to figure out how to get the sleigh out. When I freed the team, the tongue of the sleigh came to rest on the ice, and sticking out of the water. This was lucky as it gave me something to hook onto, but with what? My logging chain was on the sleigh under the water. I told McLeod to go back to the hay camp and see what he could find in the way of chains or rope, and maybe an old axe. I knew it would take him an hour or so as the haycamp was about two miles back, so while he was away I got busy.

I tried to get the team onto solid ice. I backtracked along the cutbank one horse at a time, then I took one horse and led him all over the ice to see if it would hold. I found a place that I thought was strong enough, but it was still a hundred feet or so away from the sleigh.

When Mac returned he had found an old axe and some rope, but nothing long enough or strong enough to pull out the sleigh. I cut two poplars with the axe and tied them end to end, then slid them out to the sleigh, they weren't long enough. So I cut another one, and used the halter shanks to tie them together, now they were long enough, so I used the other halter shank to tie the butt end of the poplar to the tongue. Then we used the britching straps to tie the double trees to the end of the poplar tree, and we were all set.

In this way we managed to get the front end of the sleigh up onto the ice, but we couldn't get the whole sleigh up. So there was nothing else to do but unload all we could reach. We packed it all over to where we knew the ice was strong enough, and tried to pull the sleigh out again. This time we were successful and snaked it over to solid ice.

We set out the parcels of freight separately on the ice to freeze, this way they wouldn't soak up so much water. We hitched up the team to the sleigh, ditched the wet hay, and taking our bedrolls and the grub box, went back to the haycamp for some fresh hay.

We couldn't get up the bank with the sleigh, so we left it on the river and packed up the bedrolls and the grub box. We gave the team hay and put their blankets on, they were soaking wet, but this was the best way to dry them out. We made a fire and dried out our bedtarps, fortunately our bedrolls were quite dry. Practically everything in our grub box was O.K., though the bannock had started to soak up, this was easily dried out in front of the fire.

After supper we packed hay down to the sleighs, so that we would be ready to leave early in the morning. The freight was frozen solid, we loaded it, and got away early; just as we were leaving McLeod said,

"Where is my .22 rifle?"

I asked him where he'd had it last, and he said he was holding it when we broke through the ice, I told him he couldn't have been holding it tightly enough, it must be at the bottom of the river now. I asked him if he wanted to go back and dive for it!

"No thankyou," he said, "I've had enough of that hole!" So away we went arriving at Rainbow without further trouble.

CHAPTER TWENTY-THREE

Land is Open For Filing
and Tragedy Strikes

I was on my way home from Edmonton when I heard that land was open for filing at Keg River. When I arrived home I told Fred to get on with the haying as fast as he could so that he could come with me to Peace River, and file on the land he was living on. When Allie heard the news he decided to come too.

We arrived in Peace River too late to go to the land office, so Allie and I went the next morning. There was no sign of Fred, so I went down to the MacNamara Hotel to find him. I then took him to the office to file on his land, paid the fee for him, and gave him a return boat ticket. Allie filed on the quarter closest to the river, that suited me fine, as I had had enough of watering cows down at the river. Allie and I went on to Edmonton, and on the way home we discussed the idea of growing some oats. Allie thought there should be an old disc at his place.

We had half a day to wait for the boat, so we borrowed an old Model T Ford from McKinnon and went up to Allie's old farm. Sure enough there was an old horse disc, and all kinds of machinery that hadn't been used for years, which would be of use to us if we could get it to the Keg. I got McKinnon to take the disc to the boat for me, with three sacks of oats for seed.

I had finished building at the river by now, but now I had to start building a house on my homestead. I had to get the logs out by myself, I didn't have many cows to feed so I hauled hay one day, and cut logs the next. I cut about eighty logs, and had to get Louise to help me load them on the sleigh, then I would haul them three miles up to the homestead, this took me all winter.

Coming back from Edmonton on the boat, after settling up with the Hudson's Bay Company when they took over Lamson and Hubbard, I met Sheridan Lawrence and the Government Doctor, a Miss Percy from England. Miss Percy had a team waiting for her at the landing, and Sheridan and I loaded the wagon for her with an assortment of trunks and suitcases, and away she went overland to Battle River.

This was the summer of 1929, and the last year the D. A. Thomas ran on the Peace, Allie, Louise, the boys, and I travelled out on her. Louise took the boys to stay with their Grandma where they were to go to school that winter. Later the Thomas was taken over the Vermilion Chutes by Captain Catenhead and Louis Bourassa, to be used on the Great Slave Lake. It was used there for a while though proved to be useless, as it had been built with a flat bottom for river use, and on the lake it pitched and tossed too much, so was hauled up on the bank and left to rot.

There wasn't much freight moving that year and the boats weren't leaving on schedule, when Louise came back we would have had a week to wait so I bought a little scow, loaded it up, and set out with Allie and Louise. On the way the wind got up and the waves got big, and we thought we would have to tie up, but it soon calmed down and we arrived safely. I pulled the scow up on the beach with the team, as I intended to use the lumber to build a veranda on the side of my house.

Louise was pregnant, and expecting our baby at the beginning of October. I wanted her to go out on the boat and stay in Dr. Brander's small private hospital in Edmonton, but Louise didn't want to go, she wanted Dr. Hamman to come in from the Fort. I tried to arrange this, but I found that Dr. Hamman was in Edmonton with his own wife, who had a nervous breakdown and died in Edmonton. He sent a message to say that he would be arriving at the river landing on the first of October as he would be flying in on a plane with pontoons. I waited at the landing for him for five days, then a boy came on a saddle horse to tell me to return to the Keg immediately.

I left the boy to bring my team, and I rode his saddle horse returning home through the night. Louise had had a son with the aid of the native women from the village, but she was feeling very ill. I nursed her as best I could and made every effort to get help.

In those days we had no two-way radio, and no telegraph as yet. The only way to get a message out was overland. I had to find a native who was willing to go, grub stake him, and give him money, and I didn't know if he would deliver my message, or go and get drunk first. There was a lot of delay before Dr. Hamman, whose plane had had to go to Ft. McMurray, returned to the Fort and came overland to the Keg by team.

Louise had a nervous breakdown, and didn't get any better, so he decided she ought to have treatment in hospital. We sent a messenger two hundred miles overland to Inspector Radcliffe in Peace River, asking him to phone from Peace River to Edmonton, asking for a plane to fly Louise out. Their reply would be broadcast on the radio. We got a reply in three days, so the messenger wasted no time. Wop May would be at Keg River the next day with his plane. I marked out a place at the homestead with tarp for him to land.

I told Louise that Dr. Hamman was taking her out to Edmonton, she didn't want to go, she had no faith in 'outside'. She said, "I'll never be back." She was sure she would get better with me looking after her. She was very upset when she realized that I wouldn't be able to go with her for the plane would be fully loaded, but finally I quietened her down and persuaded her to take the doctor's advice.

I wrapped her up in new Hudson's Bay blankets, and took her up to the homestead where the plane landed. I gave Dr. Hamman the baby to hold, he would hand him over to Dr. Brander who would get my mother-in-law to come and take him. I helped Louise into the plane and said goodbye to her. It was about two weeks later that a message was broadcast over the radio telling me that Louise had died in hospital.

I thought that I was doing the best thing for Louise in sending her outside to hospital, but maybe she would have been better off at home. Her death was a disaster. Apart from anything else, she was so efficient, she could do almost anything. Frank Junior stayed with his grandparents and was raised by them in Ferintosh where he runs the general store there today, and incidentally one of his friends is Denny May, the son of Wop May.

Johnny Nelson got married and filed on a homestead, this meant that Dick needed a new trapping partner, and he brought a man called Jonesy, a war veteran with his left arm missing. Dick, Jonesy, and Harry Bowe lived in Harry's house on the Chin, trapping from there during the winter. After I lost Louise, Jonesy came and cooked for me and helped all he could. With one arm missing he was considerably handicapped, but he liked to feel that he could manage anything, and he almost did. When he left he suggested that I ask Bert Gower to come up and help me.

Bert lived in Peace River up on the hill, he was a very refined gentleman who came out west after his discharge from the army on account of his health. The businessmen in Peace River called his place the country club! He said he would be delighted to come up to the Keg for the winter.

One day Narcise came to say Isidore was sick and couldn't get his breath. I told him to get Allie Brick and bring Isidore down and put him in the bunkhouse where we could look after him. We thought he had pneumonia, they brought him down right away and Allie stayed to look after him. About ten o'clock that night Allie came to the house to get some soup, and when he got back to the bunkhouse Isidore had disappeared. We went out to look for him, and found him down in the garden by the river, he had a little fire going and was sitting over it. He told Allie that he couldn't get his breath in the house. We finally managed to get him back to the bunkhouse, and I brought Allie some food and my eiderdown, so that he could stay and watch Isidore.

The next day Isidore couldn't take any nourishment, John Cardinal from the Fort came to sit with him and he pounded a drum and sang all day! Still the old man wouldn't take anything, and the next day he was so delirious, John had to hold him down in bed. There was some good in this as he couldn't pound the drum, and if he wasn't pounding that drum, he couldn't sing. The next day Isidore passed away, this was sad, he was a fine old man and a marvellous hunter. Allie saw to the burial, Isidore was the last person to be buried in the old Hudson's Bay burial ground. As Dick Hutchings said,

"He sure was a good Indian!"

When Jonesy came back on the boat he brought a partner called Andy Murphy, he had three dogs for a dog team, they were all alike, part wolfhound and very good looking dogs. Bert Gower was there, and we warehoused the freight and loaded what we could haul. I rustled up a man to take Andy and Jonesy out to their cabin on the Chin, there was a trail of sorts out there but it took a team all day to make it.

We'd had a big chinook, it took all the snow off the prairie leaving it under water, the cows were anxious to get out so I let them out to rustle for themselves. The chinook lasted a week or so, then I had to get the cows home as the prairie was all ice, I had to chop a trail for them.

McCarthy, the Provincial Policeman came in from the Fort, with Joe Kemp in attendance as Special Constable. Joe Kemp had worked for the Hudson's Bay Company for thirty years, then they fired him for some trumped up charge or other. Joe and his wife were fine people, when they left here they went to the Fort to live. McCarthy and Joe stayed at the H.B. post and Joe came down to visit me.

"What does a Special Constable do Joe?" I asked him.

"Run behind the cariole and drive the dogs, make camp, cook the supper, cook the dog's supper, feed them, clean up the supper dishes, cut spruce branches, lay out the bedrolls and so on," he said.

"What on earth possessed you to take on a job like this?" I asked him.

"When the Hudson's Bay let me go after thirty years, I couldn't find anything else and McCarthy, my brother-in-law gave me this out of the kindness of his heart." We chewed the rag, and Joe told me of some of his experiences as Special Constable, including a tale about Barney Miller. Barney built a little cabin on an island in the Peace and was supposed to be selling moonshine wholesale at the Fort. So Joe Kemp went up with McCarthy on patrol in a motor boat to check on him, this was Joe's story.

"We landed and went up to the cabin, there was Barney with four or five gallons of moonshine ready to go down to the Fort with them. McCarthy seized the jugs, and told him he was taking him to the Fort to stand trial. Barney said,

'O.K. let's go.' We all went down to the boat and Barney suddenly said, 'I've left my rifle in the cabin, I'll go and get it!' McCarthy let him go! We sat there waiting for Barney to come back, we waited for half an hour and no Barney. Finally Mac said,

'Joe, there is something wrong, you go up and see.'

'You're the policeman, you go,' I said, 'I'm not crazy enough to go and try to get a man armed with a rifle! I'll tell you what Mac, if I tip this moonshine into the river, we won't need Barney.' Mac thought that was a brilliant idea so that is what we did!

Next we went downstream and stayed at a trapper's cabin for lunch. The trapper, Shorty Doyle, was drying meat on a drying rack over a smudge.

'Shorty, you've sure got lots of meat,' said McCarthy.

'Yes I sure got a big bear,' Shorty responded. I never said a word, I knew it was buffalo! the buffalo Jim Cornwall shipped into the Buffalo Park at Ft. Smith strayed all over the place. Well Frank, I'll have to be getting back," Joe concluded.

"Be careful with all those dogs, they are liable to do anything on this glare ice." I warned him. Joe left, but within fifteen minutes the Hudson's Bay interpreter was down, he wanted me to go back with him as Joe had broken his leg just above the ankle, when putting out his foot to stop the sleigh.

I bandaged it with paper as I had no plaster of paris; paper cut in strips, when wetted and put on as tight as it will stand is a good substitute for plaster of paris, as I proved when Louis was a young boy. When Dr. Hamman at the Fort saw it, he said he would just leave it alone, as it was O.K.

A short while after this it snowed and Dr. Percy came in with the police from Notikewin she was acting as coroner. McMillan who had taken up a homestead next to Trosky, had shot himself. It looked bad at first, as the gun belonged to Trosky, but the verdict was suicide.

Usually the priest was the only one who kept track of who died and who was born, and occasionally he married people. The priest came in from the Fort in the winter by sleigh with a teamster driving him, if the snow got too deep he didn't come. He carried a little black book and wrote down who had died and who had been born since his last visit.

L'Octave (Fred) Ducharme and his wife.

Sheridan Lawrence and Allie Brick on the D. A. Thomas.

Loading cordwood on the D. A. Thomas.

Sheridan Lawrence and Frank (back to camera) helping Miss Percy load the wagon with her collection of trunks and suitcases.

View of Peace River 1928. Photo Glenbow-Alberta Institute.

The 'Sunshine' Trail Peace River 1928 — Photo Glenbow Alberta Institute.

CHAPTER TWENTY-FOUR

Settlers and First Crops

As soon as I had a homestead, I had got Pierre Gauvier, the John Deere agent in Peace River, to send me an eighteen inch walking plow. When it arrived, I took it straight down to the homestead to try it out. I used four horses and managed to plow about five acres. I disced it down, and broadcast the oats. As I had no harrow, I cut a branch of willows, and fastening a chain around them, used them as a harrow, this left the field in good shape. Then I fenced my field with a two-strand barbed wire fence.

The oats came up looking quite healthy, the first field of oats to be grown in this district! At a guess they went to about a hundred bushels to the acre. I cut them with a mower, as I had no binder, and eventually I used to thresh them with an old bedspring. I would thresh a load every night, for I had no time during the day.

As time went by I tried dumping a load in a small round corràl, and chasing some cattle round in it! This wasn't very successful, as too much manure got mixed up with the grain! I discontinued that system, and went back to the bedspring. Now I had grain I asked Charlie Rankin to save me a pig that was bred, so that I could raise some hogs.

I bought a six inch grinder from Bill Reed at Notikewin for ten dollars, but until then I cooked oats in the big cooker that I used to heat water for the calves. I acquired a second pig from a trapper, he had bought it for five dollars and that's what I gave him for it, he was glad to get rid of it, for it was costing him a lot to feed, and not getting any fatter!

I had a barrel of tar which I had got from an abandoned oilwell on the Peace, I intended to use it for roofing material. I left the barrel without a cover, and one of my milk cows decided to eat it, she seemed to relish it! She was sick for about a week, went off her food, and finally died.

I lost another milk cow that I was milking while Jonesy was with me. I always grew lots of cabbage to make sauerkraut, and after Jonesy had milked the cow, he fed her the leaves he had taken off the cabbage while making kraut. The next morning when I went to look for her she was dead.

"Whoever heard of cabbage killing a cow?" asked Jonesy.

There were no more fish, so I used the barrels for sauerkraut. The natives at Carcajou said the fish wouldn't swim through the water coming from the abandoned oil wells. It took the authorities twenty years before they capped the wells, and now the fish are returning.

Gradually other settlers came in and took up land. Trosky, the Revillon's freighter, came back with a big team of Clydesdale mares, they were a fine team, but Clydesdales are unsuitable for this country, as the mud clings to the long hair on their legs. Trosky was going to haul freight in a big way, but although he took all kinds of care of his horses, within a year they were both dead with swampfever. One had a foal before it died, but it died as a two year old. Trosky took up a homestead west of mine.

A settler came in on the boat bringing a team and wagon, intending to build a cabin on his homestead which was just north of mine. Not long after, I had a letter from the Sheriff at Peace River asking if this man was at Keg River, and if he was would I notify him. I told the man the sheriff was looking for him, he must have gone out over the trail at Ft. Vermilion. Later we decided to hay on his place and make some settlement with him if he ever came back. He never did come back, so I took a ten year lease on it.

The Government's agricultural lease meant I had to pay them so much crop off the land each year, and at the end of ten years, I could buy the land for fifteen dollars an acre. This quarter was adjoining mine, I fenced it in, and started clearing it. It was parkland with willow bluffs and poplar bluffs that had to be cleared. After a few years this lease was cancelled, the Government had a new idea. The new lease read that I had to declare how many acres I had under cultivation, and what kind of crop. I had no option on the land at all. I filled in the Government forms and sent them to Edmonton, they were returned with their share quoted, to be delivered to the Grimshaw Elevator.

I wrote to them and explained that I wanted the grain for feed. They replied that I was to pay them cash at elevator prices, instead of the grain. As the years went by, I figured out what it would cost to haul the grain out in winter, for you couldn't get over the road in summer. I had a fair idea of what it would cost for I was hauling freight over it in the winter, so I deducted this cost from the price of the grain. Sometimes they had two or three cents a bushel coming, sometimes nothing, it all depended upon the price of grain.

They kept charging me with the Grimshaw Elevator price right up to the end of my ten year lease, then it was put up for auction. I bought it, I'd had to pay for all the work I'd had done on it, but I fully expected a caveat against it for the difference I owed them on the freight of the grain if it had been hauled to Grimshaw, but there was nothing.

Jack Lane came down the river on a raft which he toppled over on the Peace, he lost all the stuff which he was bringing, though managed to save himself. He homesteaded east of my place, proved it up, and I bought it eventually.

Lonnie Root took up the homestead adjoining Allie's. Later he sold it to Dave McDonald, Emma's boyfriend. Dave trapped out west somewhere on the B.C. boundary, when he and Emma were married they lived with Allie. Dave was a first rate trapper and a good farmer. Root and Lane eventually left the district.

August La Fleur moved out to Eleske, so he told me I could hay on his hay field if I wanted to. I bought his mower and rake; his meadow was rather swampy in the early spring and always grew a fair crop of hay. August settled four or five miles out on the open hills and kept a few cattle. When he got old, and the forestry destroyed his pasture by preventing him from burning in the spring, he moved to Lower Hay.

Harry Bowe took up a homestead and built a cabin on it. McLeod took up a homestead when he came back from Rainbow, and wanted to borrow horses and plow, to plow up a piece of land for a garden. He thought I had better do it for him, as he knew nothing about plowing. I told him to take the horses out, and before he was through he would know all about it!

John Pawlowich and his wife came in over the telegraph line from Notikewin with a team and sleighs in the winter. He brought a load of worn-out machinery his father-in-law had given him for a present, this included a six foot Massey binder which John asked me to fix. I agreed to do this provided I had the use of it to cut my oats first.

Mike Yurkowsky and his family came walking into the prairie, they had come downriver on the boat looking for homesteads. They found nothing to suit them at Carcajou Point, so came to Keg River and picked out the land they wanted. Then they went out over the telegraph line, walking all the way.

The following spring Bill Halibisky came in over the telegraph line with team and sleighs, he and his wife Elsie, had a tent to live in while they built a cabin.

There was still no way to get our crops out to market when we grew them, and the settlers lived off the land. One or two of them made a little money trapping, though fur was scarce, there was little market for it and prices were low. The natives had a hard time to pay their debts, no-one had any money, so work on the telegraph line provided some cash for me, and for the men I employed.

CHAPTER TWENTY-FIVE

Right of Way for the Telegraph

During the winter of 1929-1930, the Dominion Government were cutting a right of way for the Dominion Government Telegraph between Notikewin and Ft. Vermilion. By October they were north of the First Battle River. The poplar was heavy and it all had to be cut by hand, so they were making slow progress. A Telegraph Office had been opened at Notikewin with Jack Bowie as agent.

Don Sutherland, the foreman in charge of construction, asked me if I would build a log building for the telegraph operator at Keg River. We agreed on a price of $800, and I promised to have it finished by the following spring.

Jonesy was doing the cooking for me, the boys were still with their Grandma, Fred, his boys, and Narpatches Wanuch were getting the logs out for the telegraph building, and Pete and I hauled them. Besides this I had to do chores, feed and water the cattle, saw wood and look after the store, then I got blood poisoning in my right hand and arm. This was in the days when there were no antibiotics and blood poisoning could prove quickly fatal.

I doctored it with poultices for two or three weeks, but it got worse instead of better, when the infection travelled into my shoulder I thought it was time to travel out and visit Dr. Percy at Battle River. I left Pete to do the chores and made the painful journey on my horse without stopping.

When Dr. Percy had met Sheridan Lawrence and I the previous summer, she thought she had never seen two men in better physical health, so she was surprised to see me so sick. She lanced my arm and told me how to treat it, and I told her about the problems we had had with Louise and her subsequent death. I felt sure I had sent Dr. Percy a message asking her to come, but I guess she never got it, she was sorry about this, as of the doctors we had in the country, she was the one best qualified in gynaecology.

On the way home I picked up Hilaire Minault, and we travelled together over the line that the Telegraph Co. had cut. The telegraph crew had cut about fourteen miles north of the First Battle River, and we made about five miles beyond their camp when it got too dark to find their survey, and we camped for the night. It sure was cold, we had no bedrolls, just our saddle blankets, so we had to keep a good fire going.

My arm was giving me particular hell, I steeped it in hot water and used the medicine on it, nothing helped. I was awake all the night keeping the fire going. In the morning I told Hilaire we would eat, and then go back to the doctors, for it was no use going home with an arm like this.

Dr. Percy told me that the temperature had dropped to thirty-eight below the previous night, and I must have got cold in my arm attending to it out in the open. She fixed it up again and asked me to stay over for a day or two so I went down to stay with Sandy MacLean who lived about four miles away. I stayed there for four or five days going down to the doctors every day. By then my arm was getting considerably better, so Hilaire and I set off for home once again.

My arm healed up and when we had a mild spell I was able to help Fred put up a few logs on the telegraph building. We got them high enough that we had to stand on something to reach. Fred had a barrel and I was standing on a big drygoods box that I had borrowed from the Hudson's Bay. The weight of the log in my arms was so great that the box collapsed. I came down with one leg inside the box and the other outside, with the edge of the box going up into my groin. That laid me up for two weeks, and it didn't seem to be getting any better.

Clarence Rankin was taken ill, we thought it was appendicitis, so I agreed to take him to Notikewin to see Dr. Percy, as I figured I needed some advice myself. Hilaire Minault came with us to drive the team. The stumps on the trail had been cut too high, and hidden by the snow we couldn't see them, so we gave Rankin a lot of jolts he could have done without. About thirty miles from the Keg we reached Moose Mountain which was covered with big windfall spruce. It was the middle of the night by this time, and we tore out the front bunk of the sleigh on a stump. This would have to be repaired before we could continue. Hilaire set off for the telegraph camp, which should have reached Goffit Creek by now, to get help, and I stayed to see what I could do for Rankin.

Fortunately it wasn't too cold and there wasn't much snow, so it wasn't long before Hilaire came back with a team and four men. He had sent another man ahead to Bill Reeds, to ask him to come as far as the river to meet us with his truck. The men lifted our rack onto their sleigh, and brought our sleigh to their camp to fix. We reached camp in time for breakfast, which we sure appreciated.

Rankin and I travelled to Dr. Percy's little house in Reed's truck, only to find when we got there that she was away in Edmonton. We continued on to Peace River, where I had quite a battle with the matron of the hospital before she would admit Rankin. I decided having come so far, to continue on to Edmonton, here I saw Dr. Edgar Allan who poked around for a bit but could do nothing to help me. I travelled back on the train with Dr. Percy, but at Peace River we parted company, she had a ride with a friend in a two-seater car.

I managed to get a ride to Grimshaw where I met George Robertson, he was quite a case. One of three brothers who had settled in the early days at Notikewin, and were always willing to help the new settlers in any way possible. George gave me a ride via Berwyn and Waterhole, sampling all the beer in the Peace River Country on the way.

George was trying to get a repair for his vehicle, a one-ton truck of uncertain make and vintage. Eventually we headed north for Notikewin, and everything went well until we were going down the hill close to Notikewin.

"What was that?" George asked.

"I don't know, but I saw something, and you can see the tracks in the snow," I replied. The vehicle came to an abrupt halt, and George said,

"It must have been something vital!" So we got out to see what it was.

"Why," he said, "It's our front wheel!" He went ahead to where it lay, picked it up and brought it back.

"Nothing serious," he said, "Just the bolts came out." We found three in the pile of junk that he always carried in the back and put the wheel on again.

"That will take us home again," he said, and it did. When I finally reached home I was able to tell everyone that I had seen Rankin in hospital and that he seemed to be doing fine, in spite of our rough trip.

Meanwhile the telegraph building was going up, Don Sutherland inspected it and approved it, he came in with sleighs, for the survey had got as far as Keg River, and quit for the winter, Don told us the line was expected to reach Paddle Prairie by spring.

Nearing spring he came again and told us that the camp was just on top of the hill about fourteen miles from us. We'd had a warm spell which took most of the snow, then it turned really cold. A message was broadcast over the radio from J. D. Noel, the Dominion Government Telegraph Superintendent in Edmonton, asking me to deliver it to Don Sutherland. I saddled up a horse and rode out to their camp right away.

On the way home, my horse went lame in a front leg. I thought he must have twisted it, he seemed as if he couldn't put it to the ground. I was still up on the hills, there were some fallen logs a little way back so I got my horse to them and built a fire. I thought if he rested up a little he might be able to travel again. The horse just stood by the fire, and I laid up against a big spruce tree, sleeping and keeping the fire going in between.

I woke up suddenly with a pain in my foot. I moved it around and fell asleep again, the pain became much worse and I really came alive this time. I had my foot in the fire and my sock and moccasin were burnt and smouldering! I had to find something to wrap my foot in, or it would freeze for it was very cold, so I tore up my saddle blanket in strips and wrapped my foot in that.

My horse was standing on its leg and there wasn't much swelling, I looked at it and found he had stepped on a snag which was driven up into the hoof beside the frog. What a damn fool! I should have looked at it and got it out at once. The horse was still lame but managed to carry me home. As I ate breakfast Jonesy told me that it had dropped to thirty-eight below the previous night. I told him I would have believed him if he'd told me it was a hundred below, for it sure felt like it.

As work progressed on the telegraph line, Sutherland moved his camp to Ft. Vermilion on the boat, he would work from that end which was all dry ground. This left a gap in the middle where he asked me to organize a crew to clear up the trees and build corduroys over the bogholes.

Ralph Bruger, an Austrian who trapped at Slavey Lake and was clever with cards, was foreman, Eli Danish, a Ukrainian was cook, and eight boys from the village including one of Fred's boys who was a teamster, corduroyed a piece four hundred yards long. They worked up to their waists in water all day, fighting flies besides. I had a small tent to use as a cook tent, but the men slept where they could, I paid them one dollar and twenty-five cents a day, the cook two dollars.

Don Sutherland wanted me to go out with him to Notikewin to change a piece of line around Goffit Creek. I asked him if he had a bedroll, and grub.

He had brought nothing from the camp, so I got Jonesy to bake bannock while I fixed up a bedroll. I asked Don if he had a mosquito bar.

"No what's that?" he asked.

"It's a cheesecloth tent to put over your bedroll to keep the flies out," I replied. "I will make you one, it will only take a few minutes to run one up on the sewing machine." We took a packhorse with us, and stopped where the boys were building the corduroy, they told us that our packhorse wouldn't get through packed, so Don and I carried a pack each.

Two of my crew took the horses and we jumped from one clump of rushes to another carrying the packs. I looked back to see how Don was making out, he had just jumped to a clump of rushes with his pack on his back, and the rope around his chest. When he jumped, the pack flew back and pulled him down with feet on the rushes, the rest of him almost out of sight in the mud! The boys with the horses rescued him, and when we got through was he ever mad? He wanted to build a fire right away and dry out. I finally talked him into going on, it was a hot day and I told him he would soon dry out.

We stopped at the South Keg for supper that evening and after supper I started packing up.

"What are you doing?" Don asked.

"I'm packing up, we can make another ten miles before dark," I said.

"Not another foot! I've done quite enough for one day," he said. So there I had to sit! I fixed up Don's bedroll with the mosquito bar, and he crawled into bed, it was not long before the mosquito bar was black with flies.

"This is really something," Don said, "Why didn't I get one of these long ago?"

By dark the next day, we reached Bill Reed's having made the changes to the line location on the way. Don said I could take the horses back overland, as for him, he was going to get Bill to take him to Peace River where he would get the boat, he wasn't going back over that trail again! The road was just passable by now providing it didn't rain. They were continually working on it, Floyd Kresgy worked with four mules, dragging a Fresno, a few years later he bought two Allis Chalmers cats, the first in the Peace River country.

When the corduroys were finished Don inspected them and told Ralph to keep his men on, for he had other work for them to do. On the way home we stopped in to see Harry Bowe who was working on a barn for his two horses. Don arranged with him to build a bridge on the telegraph line over the Keg for seventy-five dollars.

When the telegraph house was finished Don inspected it and approved it, then he asked me to cut out the line east from the house for three miles to meet the main line coming in from the south. He told me to cut a twenty foot clearance on the south side of the survey mounds. We had to use a team to snake the trees as they were too big to handle.

After we started I realized that we weren't on the road lines, the road lines run north and west of the survey and I was cutting south of the mounds as directed by Sutherland. I thought there must be some mistake somewhere, so I rode the seventy miles out to Don's camp to check with him. He told me it was O.K., I was to go ahead.

I made a special journey to Edmonton to see J. D. Noel, I submitted the vouchers which Don had given me for the work I had done, mentioned the new work I was doing, and the fact that it was off the road lines.

122

"I know that," he said, "We are not cutting roads for the Provincial Government!" I thought it was a waste of money for them both to cut lines when one would do, so I suggested that if he got in touch with the Province they might be willing to pay part of the cost, for the roads had to be cut out eventually. He didn't think they would, but told me to go down and see a Mr. McPherson, and see what I could accomplish. I made my suggestion to Mr. McPherson who said,

"Do you know what you are suggesting? You are suggesting that we help the telegraph people to cut their right of way, which we are not going to do?" I could get nowhere with him.

I reported back to Mr. Noel who wasn't surprised. He had Mr. Sims, the head of the Dominion Government Telegraph from Ottawa, in the office, wanting to know why the line wasn't connected up. I left them to it, but on the way home I was coming out of the bank in Peace River, when who should I see but Mr. Noel. He told me that Mr. Sims had sent him to inspect the line, and suggested that I took him over it. I told Mr. Noel it would be impossible for him to make that trip.

"I don't intend to, I'm going to Ft. Vermilion on the boat, and you can inspect the line and bring me a report at the Fort," he told me. That was a tall order for it would mean a ride of about five hundred miles by the time I had returned to the Keg, and I was supposed to be haying. However, I did as he asked, and Mr. Noel was really satisfied with my report, I was paid one hundred and fifty dollars for it.

I received eighteen hundred dollars for the six miles of line cut, and it had cost me around fifteen hundred I had paid out in trade from the store. I gave the boys ten dollars bonus. This doesn't sound so much today, but in those days it bought a pair of pants, and a shirt, and a pair of mitts.

When the muskegs were frozen, Don Sutherland called in on his way to Notikewin to make arrangements for poles and line. He was going to put up markers where he wanted the wire left along the line. The wire was number nine, running about four hundred pounds to the mile. It was given out to any farmer that wanted the job of hauling it. The snow got deep and they had to break trail. Most of them tried to haul too big a load and had to leave some and go back for it. Cabins were built to give them somehwere to camp. They were divided into two, one-half big enough for a team. There was one at Goffit Creek, and one at the South Keg. I don't know how much they were paid for hauling wire, but whatever it was, they sure earned their money.

CHAPTER TWENTY-SIX

Crossing the Battle on the Telegraph Line

When spring came Don Sutherland came in and asked me to continue cutting the line from where I had left off the previous fall. Mr. Noel wasn't satisfied with the surveying which had cost three hundred and fifty dollars a mile. I figured we would have been better without them altogether. However, I was asked to survey the route before I took a crew out to cut it. I agreed to do this, after the ground had thawed out and dried up a little, and I was to put in four foot stakes all down the prairie where the poles were to go.

Before I did this there was a message over the radio which Mr. Noel asked me to take to the pole-cutting crew. I wrote the message down and set off to deliver it to the crew who were camped at Goffit Creek sixty miles from the Keg. I rode and took a packhorse, when I got to Goffit Creek there was no-one there. I could see by the tracks that they had left that morning by wagon. I camped for the night figuring I could catch them in the morning at Notikewin.

I left early getting to the First Battle which was so full, it was almost a torrent. As I had never seen this river in such a state, I didn't know if I should tackle it. However, I saw wagon tracks where they went in, but to be on the safe side, I picketed my packhorse before I started across. I didn't get far, the water came up to my horse's belly, and he could hardly keep his feet, so I slid off him and caught hold of his tail so that he could pull me across, he made another step into deep water and over he went. I scrabbled back to shore, the horse couldn't regain his feet, and rolled over and over. Sometimes his legs were in the air, sometimes his head. He was going downstream at quite a speed, finally he washed up on a sandbar, got to his feet and whinnied. The packhorse answered him, so I thought that he would come back to this side of the river as most of the current was on the other side of the sandbar. No, he took to the water again.

It was deep water, he swam this then tried to climb the bank which was too steep and icy. He slipped back into the river, which completely covered him, he tried two or three times to get out with no success, going a little bit further downstream with every try. I saw that if I didn't get around to help him he would drown, as just below where he was trying to get out there was a cut bank where it was impossible to get out. I ran back upstream looking for a log to roll into the river and try to cross on, there were plenty of logs but they were all rotten. Then I came to the telegraph line which crossed the river. I would cross the river by the line!

125

I had shot a goose, so I rolled it in my coat, tied it up and climbed the pole. I went over the wire, what a sensation! As I got to the middle of the river the wire gave a violent jerk, and I thought the whole thing was collapsing and about to dump me in the boiling water below. However, all that had happened was that my weight had pulled up the slack on the line. Looking up the hill I saw that we were still in line with the poles, everything was still under control, and I kept on going. I got across and down the pole safely. One word of advice, if you ever have to do this wear some leather pants for the splinters that those climbing spurs make are not at all nice to slide down over, they are most uncomfortable!

I ran down the river, cut across the point where I could see down the river for half a mile, no horse. I couldn't see how he could have got out of sight in such a short time. I came back following the river but seeing no sign of him. I crawled down to where he had tried to get out and there I found all kinds of boot tracks, which made me wonder what had happened. I looked for wagon wheel tracks coming out of the river, there were none, so I concluded that they had got into some difficulties. I then headed down the trail for Notikewin.

Bill Reed wasn't at home, so I stopped in at a homesteader's shack, a bachelor by the name of Norman Filleau, I had coffee with him and told him about losing my horse in the river. He said when he went down the next day to hunt for rats he would keep a lookout for it. I told him if he should find it dead to try and get the saddle off it, for it was a hundred and fifty dollar saddle, I also told him there was a rope at the foot of the telegraph pole if he needed it.

I then went on to the Second Battle. Across the river I saw old Bob Biswanger on a little raft, loading up some household goods belonging to a settler named Hart, who had wintered in a little cabin on the river belonging to Bob.

Bob Biswanger was an expert shot, because he had only one arm and couldn't handle a rifle, he was allowed to carry a revolver. The settlers had a bathtub full of dishes and a pile of other stuff loaded on the raft ready to go. I waited for them to come across so that I could have a ride back with Bob. Old Bob was standing on the raft with a long pole ready to push off. I yelled to Bob to sit down, but he took no notice, I yelled again, but he pushed the raft out and over it went, dumping everything in the river.

They got old Bob out of the water and raced downstream trying to save the things that floated. I found an old rail fence, put it in the river, and shot across the river on it. The river was only about fifty feet wide and the current was not as strong as at the First Battle. I told Bob my story, and he said that five men had been through the day before, and gone towards Notikewin.

I said Goodbye to Bob and went on to Joe Rousseau's store. Here I found the crew and delivered my message. Then I asked them what had happened to their team and wagon. They said they thought the water was shallow, so drove them in, then the team stepped into deep water and were swept off their feet. They would have rolled over but the wagon prevented that, the men all jumped off, and the rack came loose from the wagon and started floating away down the river, they tried to catch it but it was impossible. They couldn't rescue the team and wagon either so walked into

Notikewin. I told them my story, and they thought that I wouldn't see my horse again.

Louis Bourassa had the mail contract that winter, and he took three English ladies to Ft. Vermilion by the river route, down the First Battle, to where it joined the Peace, and on this trip they found the crew's team hung up on the boulders, the carcasses still in harness and hitched to the wagon.

Sandy MacLean came in and gave me a ride down to the doctors in his 480 Chev, an open touring car, it was only about four miles but it took over an hour to make it, and I didn't get much of a ride as I was pushing that Chev through the mud for most of the way. I presented the Doctor with the goose and had tea with her, then I had to go back to see to my horse that I had left picketed.

Sandy and I repeated the same performance, Sandy driving and me pushing. Then I went to the store and bought two cotton clothes lines and a dozen six inch spikes. I stayed the night with Sandy, the next morning he said he would like to drive me to the river, but the road was getting worse. I told him I would rather walk than push that Chev.

At the Second Battle I crossed on the raft, then I went to Norman Filleau's cabin, he had just finished breakfast and cooked me some hot cakes. He had found my horse up to his neck in the river and managed to fish up his bridle lines and pull him upriver to where he could get out. He was exhausted, but Norman put the blanket on him after he'd taken the saddle off, and he had lots of grass to eat. The picketed horse saw him and they whinnied to each other having quite a conversation.

I thanked Norman and gave him an order for $25 on Joe Rousseau's store, which he told me later, grub-staked him through the winter. At the river I found my saddle-horse and saddle. I saddled it up and then drove my spikes up the pole. I tied my clothes lines to the bridle reins, took my horse as close to the river as I could and placed a rock on the lines so as to hold my horse, I then climbed the pole holding the line, half-way over there was enough slack in the line, so that it dragged in the water, which got worse the further I went. I was scared it would pull my horse loose, though I was lucky, it held.

I made all the speed I could down the pole, it still held, I started to pull it in, it came out of the water though I couldn't get it loose from the rock, I had the bridle lines pulled tight with the horse's head right down to the rock, he didn't like this and gave a jerk which turned him loose from the rock. I kept pulling as much as I thought the line would stand, and the horse finally came to the river and started across. I kept his head pulled upstream, and he made it across without going downstream too far. I left him with the other horse while I climbed the pole again to put in the rest of my spikes, ready for any other time I might need them.

That should have been enough incidents for one trip but there was more to come. After twenty-five miles or so I had to camp for it was too dark to travel on that road. I ate the last of my bannock though I had plenty of tea. I made five miles or so at daylight, crossing a small muskeg when my saddle horse bogged down in a waterhole. I had to leave it and lead my packhorse around through the willows.

I had been on the telegraph line before but only in the winter when the ground was frozen, so didn't know the nature of this swamp. I found my horse had his hind feet in a hole in the ice about three feet from the surface. I could feel it with my feet, it was about two feet across with the sides rounded and smooth, I got a rail and put it down the hole and found there were ten feet of running water! It seemed the hole was made by water coming up from the stream below.

I put a bunch of dry muskeg spruce down to hold his head out of the water, then I rolled him over on his side and pulled up one hind leg until I could get a rope around it. I took the clothes line and made it fast to a clump of willows, then I put the rope through a loop on the clothes line and pulled it tight so that the foot couldn't slip back into the hole. This made the horse struggle to get up, I pulled up all the slack and he managed to get the other foot out of the hole, taking up all the slack so that he couldn't slip back, one more try and he was on his feet.

All this business must have taken two hours or more, I took him to where my packhorse was, then I went back and with a piece of charcoal, made a notice on an old board, 'Stop! Do not try to cross,' and I put it up on the edge of the swamp. This didn't help, two natives driving a team on their way to visit Antoine Beaulieu later on in the summer, ignored the warning, if they could read it, drove straight in and drowned their team.

Antoine was away hunting but his kids let me have a little bannock. At the South Keg, I rested the horses, and from there I made home through the night, hoping I would never have to make another trip like that!

Paul More, the Telegraph Agent, came with team and democrat full of equipment for the office. Bill Halibisky came looking for a sack of potatoes to plant, and I asked him if he wanted a job on the telegraph line, helping me to survey it, he said he would. We took a tent and grub for a week, and with one of Fred Ducharme's boys as helper, we staked out twenty miles, leaving a stake for each pole, we had to have a crew before we could continue, so returned home.

We soon got a team of seven men together, Bert baked bannock and we put the grub up. In those days there was nothing fancy, we took five sacks of potatoes, tea, sugar, meat, dried prunes and apples, flour, baking powder, lard, twenty pounds of golden syrup, for the boys liked hot cakes, and I sent a two gallon crock of mustard pickles that I had put up myself. The seven men loaded up their beds, tents, tables and stores, and I followed on my saddlehorse.

Bill and I started the survey next morning, we cut one try-line and ran into big spruce, I didn't want to cut this, so wavered towards the Paddle Creek and got out of the big timber, though this meant we would have to get north to get back in line. By dark we had the line well started so the men could start cutting.

I left Bill as foreman and Eli Danish to haul logs, all the cutting was done by hand in those days, power saws were not thought of as yet. I went back to surveying, and while I was doing this Don Sutherland showed up, he seemed to be satisfied with what we had done, we had the prairie staked out for twenty miles. I surveyed for ten miles which I thought would take the men a week to cut and I went home to butcher a cow so that I could send meat down for the men, probably one of the boys would get a moose in the meantime.

128

After I butchered, I sent meat down to the camp and got busy canning the rest. I had plenty of sealers, Louise had had them full of wild berries such as blueberries, saskatoons, cranberries, raspberries and black currants. We had used these all up, so I filled two hundred quart sealers with meat, boiling the bones in my big cooker for the soup, then boiling the sealers forty at a time.

I went back to the camp with more meat, tobacco, and matches, packing a saddle horse for Bill to ride as it was too far to walk from camp to where we were surveying. The cook complained that he now had too much fresh meat, so I told him to put it under water in the shade, where the sun didn't shine on it and it would keep for a month.

Bill and I went ahead with the survey and worked on it for about two weeks, then one morning we saw movement on the edge of the bush across an opening in the bush which opened onto a small prairie. We watched for a while and saw some men, so went over to see what it was. It was Sutherland's survey crew with old Abbita as guide, their camp was back about seven miles. So we had done well to come out opposite Sutherland's survey.

We connected up the line the next day, Don said, he had not expected us to meet so close. He was going to move his camp back to Notikewin to put in piles and string wire. I told him of the water-hole I had got into, and he said he would see what he could do about it when he got there. Bill Halibisky agreed to stay on the job and see it through, we moved the camp away ahead so that they could work both ways from the camp, then I went home and sent more supplies including beef and tobacco. Eventually we wound up work on the telegraph line. I inspected the line, and paid off the men. I gave the men a ten dollar bonus and they were all satisfied.

Walking plow — Keg River.

The telegraph camp near Notikewin, 1929.

The first car to drive to Keg River (helped up the hill with a team)!

'Young' Frank at Ferintosh.

Art, Frank and Louis.

Oil well in Peace River area. Photo Glenbow-Alberta Institute.

132

Abandoned oil well near Peace River town, 1933 — Photo Glenbow-Alberta Institute.

Dovetailing on the Telegraph House.

CHAPTER TWENTY-SEVEN

Travels to Notikewin

The boys wanted to come home, so I went to fetch them. On the way, I stopped at the Telegraph camp and collected up Ted Amos, their camp cook. He had burnt his fingers while lighting a gas lamp and bound them with friction tape to keep the water out while he washed dishes. I insisted that he come with me to see Dr. Percy. She treated his hands for a few days until they began to heal, then sent him back with a pair of rubber gloves to wear while washing dishes!

We had turned the horses loose in Henry Letander's pasture and walked over to Sandy McLean's, Sandy drove us to Doctor Percy's house, there were planks covering a big mud-hole but we managed to stay on them. Dr. Percy's little house was five miles from Notikewin, the first house to be built where the town of Manning is now.

I had previously bought a '29 Chev coupe from Jim Robertson, George's brother, Jim had acquired it in trade for a load of lumber he'd got while working at the mill. Money was short and he'd thought the car would be easier to sell than the lumber. I couldn't drive it home, but I thought it would be useful to me if I could drive to Peace River in it, so I bought it and left it with Dr. Percy, she could use it whenever possible and on this occasion she drove me to Peace River in it.

In Edmonton I hired a car and went down for the boys. When I told them I was taking them home, and that I had left their horses in Notikewin, they were in a rush to go and got their things together at once. Little Frank had sure grown and wanted to come too but I had to leave him. We had supper at Joe Hong's Chinese Restaurant at Notikewin and camped at Henry Letanders for the night. After supper the boys stayed with the Letander boys while I went down to visit Dr. Percy.

Crossing the First Battle River, we met Dan Landry for the first time. He was building a house for his wife and family of one girl and three boys, he intended to trap up and down the river. One spring I stopped in at his place and he showed me two baby deer, three days old, asleep in the bedroom. The old doe hearing us talking came bounding in through the open window to see what was going on. Dan had caught the doe when it was small two years before, he kept a large red ribbon round its neck, hoping to protect it from the hunters, but someone shot it the following fall. Dan built me a small warehouse at the river, and a place to keep my car. In time to come he proved to be a great help to the freighters using the telegraph line, for he used to double up with them on the hill with his team.

More and more people began to use the telegraph line especially in the winter when there was good sleighing. Jack Haywood, the R.C.M.P. officer from Notikewin came in to round up the local moonshiners. They succeeded in getting two, swore me in as Justice of the Peace, and fined them ten dollars as it was their first offence. It wasn't their first offence by any means, but it was the first time they had been caught!

After haying Fred brought one mower home as he was going to cut some hay for himself, he thought he could get some on the little prairie across the Keg River. He took the mower and put his own team on it, one was a roan stallion, and about as mean as he could be. Fred left them standing and the stud took off after a loose horse, the men chased after them but the machine was in gear, so they were afraid to get too close. When they finally caught the horses the machine was a complete wreck and smashed beyond fixing, for we had no welding plants as yet.

However, I did manage to fix up John Pawlowich's old binder. I replaced the leather bindings and made a new table with galvanized iron, for the table was all rotten, and the boxes worn out. I managed to repair enough canvases for a set, though they would need careful handling to last the season.

On my next trip out I bought a new packer needle and some new sections for the sickle knife. I worked on this machine for two weeks before it looked something like a binder. After we'd finished haying, it took me four days to cut my oats with John's binder. The boys and I threshed oats, pounding out a load a day, and feeding the straw to the cows. We now took oat bundles with us on the trail for feed, as they were so much better than baled hay and easier to load.

Our grinder was too slow, so I bought an eight inch one on my next trip out. When hooked up to the Fordson, we really made headway, and appreciated it after the little grinder and one-horse engine we had struggled with for so long.

We harvested potatoes and cabbages from the garden taking up fifty sacks of potatoes from less than a quarter of an acre. Fifty-four big potatoes filled a sack. I have never seen ground that produced potatoes like that at Keg River, in later years my son-in-law Johnny Vos, produced up to a thousand bushels of potatoes an acre on it. At Keg River Crossing, John Christian grew the biggest cabbages I have ever seen. We stacked our cabbages in the meat-house until Emma had time to make sauerkraut for us.

More homesteaders were coming in, the Schimeluks with three fine horses and a heap of effects. The Yukowskis with two boys, a team, wagon and sundry things. They were the Ukrainians who had been in the previous summer and taken up homesteads, their daughters were married to John Pawlowich and Bill Halibisky.

The horses they brought with them all died shortly after with swamp fever. One of my mares got swamp fever one spring, and I turned her loose on the prairie with the other horses to die. She didn't die, and late in the fall I saw her with the other horses, she was as fat as she could get, so I caught her up and took her on a trip to the river in a four horse team hauling freight. On the way back she played out completely, she went back to skin and bone, it was incredible to see her shrink to nothing on one trip. When we got home I turned her loose again and that was the last I saw of her, she must have died in the bush somewhere.

136

There wasn't much to do in the store for no-one had any money, and fur prices were dropping all the time. As Pete said, fur was hardly worth catching, red fox down to three dollars, coyote to two dollars, weasel ten cents and up, and squirrel only ten cents. It was difficult for any trapper to pay his debts and we were lucky if the moonshiners dldn't get it first.

When John Christian and Blackbird came in they had a bunch of John's kids with them, they had brought squirrel and weasel to trade for candy. John's wife could speak a little English with which she communicated with John, but she spoke only Cree to the kids, therefore John couldn't understand his own kids, and when they were in the store I would interpret for him as by now, I could speak a little Cree.

It was closed season on beaver, the traders bought them anyway but they would have had them confiscated if they were caught. Fur runs in cycles, and whether the season is open or closed makes no difference as I told the Game Commissioner when I met him in Edmonton. He told me that he had nothing to do with it, the Government told him what to do! About this time there were millions of rabbits in Central Alberta, and traders were paying 3¢ a skin for them, three carloads went out from Wetaskiwin, and the Game Commissioner was told to close the season on rabbits! The following year the rabbits all died off as they do at the end of their cycle; bureaucrats will make these decisions!

Joe Kemp had been given the job of postmaster at the Fort, so when Joe McCarthy the Provincial Policeman came in Tommy Bourassa was driving him. They stayed at the Hudson's Bay Post and I asked Tommy the purpose of their visit. When he told me they were checking up on beaver, I ran up my flag as a warning to the trappers that the police were in! When McCarthy came into my yard he said,

"Frank, I will have to lay a charge against you!"

"Oh," I said, "What is it?"

"For defacing the Canadian flag," he replied. It was the red ensign, with the letters K.R.T.C. sewn on it in patches.

"That's news to me," I said, "Go ahead and give me the summons, I will keep it as proof of your ignorance, for Canada hasn't got a flag, that flag is the red ensign and doesn't count." Finally he left muttering that he would have to get advice on the matter.

Later Tommy asked me if he'd searched the store. I laughed, "No, he was too much blown up about my flag!" I told him.

It was time to take my fur out to sell, it took me two days to reach Notikewin with four saddle horses and two packhorses. There was no-one at Antoine's cabin, and they had all gone to bed at Dan Landrys.

We turned our horses loose in Henry Letander's pasture and camped there. I left the boys to eat at Joe Hongs and amuse themselves with Henry's boys who were about the same age, and Sandy McLean drove me to Dr. Percy's to pick up my car. I took my fur to Martin Wener in Peace River who persuaded me to go to Edmonton with him. We had the back of the car loaded down with fur, and we made a good trip even though the road was still only a wagon trail in places, it took us twenty-four hours going by Athabasca. I stayed with the Weners who were living in Strathcona, and I talked long into the evening with old Max Wener who was a fine old man.

Back in Peace River again, I had supper with Osborne Lawrence, after supper he suddenly remembered that he had two cows to milk. He had bought one milk cow at an auction for twenty-seven dollars, someone had bid twenty on the next cow, so Osborne bid twenty-two to help the sale along and found himself the owner of a second milk cow.

"What are things coming to?" he asked, "Wheat is only twenty cents, oats eleven or twelve cents, butter fifteen cents, and eggs, you can't give away!"

Dr. Percy told me that Ted Wanes wanted to sell his homestead for five hundred dollars, she was thinking of buying it and asked my advice. I was considering it as a farm, and as such I told her it wasn't worth two bits, there was nowhere to make a decent field it was just up and down gravel ridges.

"If you've got five hundred dollars to throw away," I told her, "Throw it in the river, that will save you a lot of headaches though who's to know?" This homestead was where the town of Manning is today!

Joe Rousseau, the store keeper asked me if I would like to buy some butter, he had taken it from farmers and couldn't sell it. He thought I could use it for dog grease! I bought a hundred pounds from him for ten dollars! I packed it in a rawhide pannier, where it melted a little and the papers got mixed up in it. Emma sorted it out and packed it up again and it was perfectly good butter, which I sold in the store.

When we stopped at Bill Reeds to ask him to pick up some machinery I had bought in Peace River, he said he was trying to buy a bigger truck to haul grain as the roads were getting better, but with wheat at only twenty cents plus the expense of hauling it wasn't very profitable.

Don Sutherland sent in a message from the telegraph camp asking me to take out an injured man. Ralph Lorenzon had failed to jump back far enough while felling a big spruce and got his leg pinned against the stump. It was badly bruised and swollen, though it did not seem to be broken. I instructed them to make a box about three feet long, we bandaged the knee with cotton batting and strips of blanket, then we bandaged the whole leg including the foot to keep it from getting cold and stuffed it in the box with bandages so that it couldn't move. After that we bandaged over the whole thing to keep the box on the leg. We sent a wire to Bowie to get Bill Reed to meet us at the river, from there we took him to the Doctor and she sent him on to Peace River with Bill in his truck, and I visited with the Doctor!

I finally ran out of excuses to visit Notikewin, I had no machinery to bring in and no injured man to take out, so I got Emma to come up and stay with the boys and I went with my dog team to visit Dr. Mary Percy. I still had my dog team though they were not in such good shape as when Bert was looking after them. Bill Lambert had borrowed them and when he brought them back he said they tired out quickly, so I gave them a couple of day's rest before I set out. We got half-way to Notikewin before they played out and I made camp for the night.

After I got my fire going a man came walking up the line, he was camped just over the hill and his name was Mike Rudy. His wife and family of five boys and a girl were with him, he had two teams and came from Dauphin, Manitoba, the Schimeluks had advised them to come.

"What a desolate country!" he said, "I have a notion to turn back."

"What did you do with your farm in Dauphin?" I asked him.

138

"I sold it," he admitted.

"Then you've nothing to go back for," I told him.

"No that's the trouble," he said. He had brought a car of settlers' effects to Grimshaw and had hauled his machinery as far as Notikewin leaving his two milk cows with a farmer in Notikewin for the winter. He thought he might have to take his horses back if he couldn't get enough feed for them at Keg River. I did my best to cheer him up.

I left at daylight, but they were all asleep at Rudy's camp as I passed. I arrived at Dr. Percy's by dark.

"You have come just in time," she said, "I have a call to Bill Fedorchuk's place about three miles away."

"What's wrong?" I asked her.

"Nothing's wrong, it's a maternity case, but there's no rush, have some supper first, "Then you can take me over with the dogs."

It was really cold and I had to stay outside as the cabin had only one room. I got some hay to bed the dogs down, crawled into my eiderdown and went to sleep. I don't know how long I was asleep, but it was still dark when Bill Fedorchuk came out and told me the baby had arrived. I looked around for my dogs, and all I could see was chewed up harness.

Bill hunted up some baling wire to patch up my harness and I hunted up my dogs, which I found bedded down in the haystack. It was lucky they hadn't decided to go home. It took me all the next day to mend my harness. The next morning I set off for home, and as it was brilliant moonlight I travelled all night as well, making camp from time to time to rest the dogs.

I went back to threshing oats, my pigs had done well so we butchered two hogs giving us fresh meat and bacon. The five left were all female and being close to the end of December I put them all in with the boar, this gave me six breeding pigs counting the old sow.

I had bought a Massey Harris four run single disc drill which I thought was the best for our district, so I had to go to Notikewin to haul it, this gave me another opportunity to visit Dr. Mary Percy! Bill Reed helped me load the drill which was heavier than I thought, it weighed about a ton and was almost too heavy for one team over that trail, I wished I had four up. I got Dan Landry to double up with me on the hill at the Battle and made home in two days and a night.

Pete wanted to visit the Fort and I asked him if he had a girl down there.

"No," he said, "They don't interest me," maybe he was telling the truth for he never married. Bill Reed had cleaned ten sacks of garnet wheat for me, which he had grown, and I told Pete when I wanted to go and fetch it.

"How would it be if I went for the wheat?" asked Pete.

"No, I have some personal business to attend to," I told him.

"Yes," said Pete, "Some monkey business I'll bet!" I took Allie's team as I had shod them, I made Landrys the second night, and Bill's the next day. I put up my team and Bill took me down to the Doctor's place.

Mary was home and we had a lively evening together, before it was over we had decided to get married. The next day we went to Peace River to get the ring and the necessary papers. The road was fairly good, packed hard by the farmers hauling grain to the elevator at Grimshaw with teams. I remembered to get grain bags from the flour mill for my wheat, and we returned the next day. That night we went to visit Jack Hayward the

139

R.C.M.P. officer in charge of the district. He and his wife lived in a little log cabin across the river, the second house to be built in Manning, and they gladly agreed to stand up for us. The following evening Mr. Parker the United Church Minister married us, the ceremony concluded, we stayed for lunch and went home.

Mary had to give a month's notice to the Government before she could leave Notikewin, so the next morning she drove me back to Bill Reeds, and then went back to work out her notice.

Bill and I loaded the wheat, and I paid Bill a dollar a sack for it, he thought that was too much, but I didn't agree for he had surely made a good job of cleaning it. I told Bill I would be back at the end of the month to pick up my wife.

"Yes," said Bill, "We've been expecting it!" I got home in two days.

"Did you bring the wheat?" asked Pete, "Or did you forget it?"

"No," I said, "I remembered everything, even to getting married!"

"Yes," said Pete, "You wouldn't listen to me when I told you to keep out of Notikewin, that shows what harm the telegraph line has done to this country, if it hadn't been cut out you would have stayed at home."

"Maybe so," I said, "But don't forget Pete, this will be the only district with a doctor who will stay, not like the Fort, that has one today, and gone tomorrow."

At the end of the month I went back to Notikewin to bring Mary home. The trail wasn't too bad for we didn't have much snow that winter. I took the team with me as we had Mary's things to bring back. On the way back we camped in the bush, and Mary got some idea of what it was like to camp for the night under the stars.

CHAPTER TWENTY-EIGHT

First Car to Keg River

I was working outside one evening when of all things a car came up to our door and stopped! I went over to find Joe Rousseau, George Robertson, and Slim Jackson. Sandy McLean was ill and had been taken to Edmonton hospital, so they had bought Sandy's old car. As the trail was still frozen, they thought it would be a good lark to make the trip to Keg River. Dan Landry had pulled them up the hill at the Battle with his team, and they hadn't had much trouble from there.

They stayed the night, with me and the next morning said they didn't think they could make the hill going south without a team to pull them up. I told them I knew that, the hill was straight up in places and was all a team could do to make it up with no load. I told them I would take a team out and pull them up the hill. It was twelve miles from home so they would have to wait for me. As it happened they got there first and couldn't resist trying to make it without help.

They couldn't get a run at it as it went up a coulee. However, they tried several times to make it, pushing and shoving. By the time I got there they had torn out the rear end and were really stuck when I arrived. They decided the best thing to do was to take my team and let me try to get their car home until they could bring repairs. I wasn't very keen on this idea, for if it didn't work I would have a twelve mile walk home!

It was downhill for miles so I would see how far I could go. We turned the car round, they gave me a push downhill and away I went driving as fast as it would go so it would jump the teeth that were torn out in the crown gear. There were water-cans, gas-cans and goodness knows what else in the back seat, and they bounced about and made a terrific noise. What with that and the racket made by the rear end you could hear me coming for miles. I drove like crazy bouncing over stumps and rattling over the two long corduroys. I made these safely and wondered about Harry Bowe's bridge, I decided that if Jim had managed to cross it on his way in it must be O.K. so I hit it as fast as I could. I drove crazily on until I hit the prairie when I slowed down too much and stalled. I pushed several times to see if it would take off but with no success. Finally Johnny Nelson saw me and came over With Harry Bowe, I got in and let them push while I tried to catch a piece of gear and eventually I made it. Off I went again and made it home without further incident. Pete thought they were a bunch of fools, and would probably kill my team.

Eventually Jim Robertson brought my team safely back bringing with him repairs for his car. He and Rankin who was up with the mail worked on it

141

together. They found that there were three teeth out in the crown gear, they were stuck to the bottom of the housing which was quite dry.

"I guess Sandy didn't think it needed oil in there!" Jim said. Jim had only brought a quart of oil so we made it up with mowing machine oil. Jim made arrangements for someone to pull him up the hill on his way out, and I told him not to try any monkey business on the hill, but to wait for a pull. I heard later that they had had no trouble at all this time.

The new settlers needed lumber, so Harry Bowe bought a tractor to operate a sawmill. The small tractor he bought was unsatisfactory so he bought a big model K cross-mounted engine, rated thirty horses on the belt. I needed lumber to build a bin for my oats and to build more pig houses before weaning time. The last of my sows came in giving me forty-eight little pigs. I had plenty of green stuff to give them after I had thinned out my garden. I also had plenty of oats for my pigs, though oats aren't the best food to fatten pigs, so I was hoping my wheat would turn out O.K. Sheridan Lawrence had grown wheat at Ft. Vermilion, but it had never been grown in this district before, so it was a bit of a gamble. However, we put in three or four acres and hoped for the best.

Meanwhile Mary had to go to Peace River to appear in court as a witness, and I had my fur to take out, so we went out together. Hilaire Minault wanted to come with us and I agreed to loan him a horse. I had about twenty head of cayuses taken in debts one way or another.

We packed the boy's horse, Dan. Dan was a real packhorse and always knew what to do. I never led him, I always left him to follow. If his pack touched a tree, he would back up and find a bigger opening. If we went through a muskeg, and it wasn't to his liking, he would go off and find a better crossing for himself.

About ten miles from home, just as we started up the hills it started to rain. We took the old trail which added twenty-five miles to our journey, but had good feed for the horses, and was better in wet weather. We camped at Stoney Creek that night and the next day we rode all day in the rain to the First Battle, and then the night we camped by the river about twelve miles from Notikewin, it was still raining and by now everything was soaking wet.

We arrived at the R.C.M.P. barracks the next night, and left the next day for Peace River with Jack Haywood. Hilaire took our horses back to Henry Letanders and turned them loose in his pasture. Mary and Jack went to the trial, I sold my fur to Marten Wener, then I went shopping and bought an eight foot McCormick binder, ten spools of barbed wire, and groceries to be shipped on the boat.

On the way home we stopped at Grimshaw and had lunch at Dan's Chinese restaurant, Jack always liked to visit Dan as he had spent his youth in China and could talk Chinese with him. At Notikewin Mary and I left Jack and headed north stopping at Joe Rousseau's store to take on some grub for the trail. We decided to go back by the telegraph line, there was poor feed for the horses and in places we had to walk through swamps up to our waists in water, but it was twenty-five miles shorter.

The second night out from Notikewin we camped at Beaulieu's old place, they had moved to the Fort so there was no-one there. It was dark when we arrived and we made supper outside. However, it looked like rain so we rolled our beds down on the floor inside the cabin. In the morning Mary said,

"There's sure a horrible smell in here." I agreed with her and went out to light the fire for breakfast. Mary appeared later saying,

"No wonder it smelled in there, I was sleeping by a dead cat!"

"That's the value of experience," I told her, "Now you'll always look before you set your bedroll down, I've had experience which is why I didn't put my bed down on that cat!"

I told her how one time when I was freighting with four others we failed to make our usual stopping place and stopped at a native cabin for the night. The other boys brought in their beds after supper, and flopped them on the floor taking up all the space.

The only open spot I could find was behind the stove, I couldn't see too well as there was only one candle. Well, I unrolled my bedroll and crawled in, what a smell! No matter for I was soon asleep, but in the morning the smell filled the cabin. It must have been a bit much even for the old lady, for she had left the door wide open. When it got lighter I saw the source of the smell. The old lady had been throwing the guts out of the rabbits behind the stove, and I had put my bedroll on top of it all!

When Mary and I reached the Keg River, we found that the rain had left it booming full. The bridge Harry Bowe had built was completely gone, and the water had cut into the bank, washing out the roots of a big spruce which had fallen into the river onto the trail where the horses had to cross the river. I crawled down the tree and chopped the top off so that the horses could pass.

We couldn't herd the horses across because they would go downstream where they couldn't get out of the river, they had to go upstream to hit the trail where they could get out. We collected all the rope we could find and joined it together, and Mary volunteered to swim across and pull the horses across the river. I sent Dan over first, and Mary pulled him up onto dry land. I told her to tie him up right there so that the other horses could see him.

Mary tried to throw the rope back to me but it kept falling in the river. Oh my! You should have heard the language, and why hadn't I sent her clothes over on Dan? I told her that if she got any more mud on her she wouldn't need clothes! She had plastered herself with mud to keep the flies and mosquitoes off which were very bad. I told her to find a pole and stay downstream, I would chase a horse in and if he headed downstream she could head him back upstream.

As it turned out this wasn't necessary, as the horse headed upstream to join Dan by himself. Mary had her clothes again, and the air started to clear, no more bad language! I followed on the other horse and piled off in the mud so that the horse could climb the bank. It was late when we got home, as we had six miles further to go after getting across the river.

It was a little over ten years since I had struggled up the trail from Carcajou with my family and all my cows; life had not been easy, and it had been a black time when Louise died but now we were a family again, and maybe things would get better. Ranching up here had not been an unqualified success but we had pulled through somehow, and next year I had plans to take all my cattle out and start a herd of Aberdeen Angus for they seemed to be a hardier breed for this part of the world.

Times were hard and no-one had any money to spend, we had no way to sell our crops, but we had enough to eat and we were all in the same boat. At least we were squatters no longer, Harry Bowe came in with the mail and brought the Homestead Inspector, I managed to persuade him that I was fulfilling my obligations with regard to living on the homestead, and he was very impressed with the crops, so maybe one day a way would be found to get our crops out to markets. The telegraph was a big boon for we could communicate with the outside world, a new telegraph operator came in with his wife and they added to our small community. We had one big advantage over many small isolated communities, we had a doctor!